only in ——————
SANTA FE

text by
SUSAN HAZEN-HAMMOND

photographs by
EDUARDO FUSS

Voyageur Press

To the memory of
Mary Scott "Scottie" King,
one of the best editors
and finest Santa Feans ever

Printed in Hong Kong
92 93 94 95 96 5 4 3 2 1

Library of Congress Cataloging-in-Publication Data
Hazen-Hammond, Susan.
Only in Santa Fe / Susan Hazen-Hammond ; photography by Eduardo
Fuss.
p. cm.
Includes bibliographical references.
ISBN 0-89658-214-0
1. Santa Fe (N.M.)—Guidebooks. I. Fuss, Eduardo, 1938- .
II. Title.
F802.S4H39 1992
917.89'560453—dc20 92-18402
CIP

Published by
VOYAGEUR PRESS, INC.
P.O. Box 338, 123 North Second Street
Stillwater, MN 55082 U.S.A.
From Minnesota and Canada 612-430-2210
Toll-free 800-888-9653

Voyageur Press books are also available at discounts for quantities for
educational, fundraising, premium, or sales-promotion use. For
details contact the marketing department. Please write or call for our free
catalog of natural history publications and a free copy of our
newsletter, *Wingbeat*.

Front cover: As the moon rises, it competes with the electric farolitos along the multi-layered roofline of the Inn at Loretto. Photographs of the adobe-style inn, built in the mid-1970s, are sometimes mistaken for Taos Pueblo.

Back cover: Artist Georgia O'Keeffe's interest in animal skulls helped make them a basic part of Santa Fe Style decor. Here, a cow skull accents a stucco wall on the patio of a westside Santa Fe home.

Page 1: Wisteria blossoms hang in front of the historic Roque Tudesqui House on East de Vargas Street. Tudesqui, born in Italy in 1801, owned this house in the early 1840s. Its adobe walls may already have been ancient then.

Page 3: Anglo, Indian, Mexican, and Spanish artisans of the Southwest have worked silver for generations. Here silver concha belts by a Santa Fe silversmith rest on a Navajo saddle blanket.

Contents

Introduction: Everybody Has Heard

▼▼▼▼▼▼▼▼▼▼▼▼▼▼▼▼▼▼▼▼▼▼▼▼▼▼▼▼▼▼

"Everybody has heard of the old palace in Santa Fé, New Mexico," wrote *Ben Hur* author Lew Wallace a century ago, after serving as governor of New Mexico Territory.

So what? his wife Susan contended. To her Santa Fe was "the sleepiest place in the world . . . dirty and unkempt, swarming with hungry dogs."

Today the dogs eat well and the city has won national recognition for its Santa Fe Beautiful campaign. Few residents live by, or even remember, the old northern New Mexico joke: "Nights are for sleeping; days are for resting." But still Santa Fe perplexes newcomers.

My own first impression of Santa Fe was that it didn't exist.

The highway sign on Interstate 25 read "Santa Fe, next three exits." I looked around, confused. To the right, juniper and piñon trees covered the low hills like mules in a pasture. Ahead, to the northeast, the Sangre de Cristo Mountains rose to thirteen thousand feet. To the left lay—well, I wasn't sure what. A few one-story, earth-colored houses with no visible roofs played peek-a-boo behind cottonwoods and poplars. But the homes faded so well into the summer landscape that there didn't seem to be enough of them to constitute a town, much less the largest city in northern New Mexico.

I didn't know the history that lay behind each of the three off ramps: Cerrillos Road, St. Francis Drive, and Old Pecos Trail. So I chose Old Pecos Trail for the Wild West sound of its name.

After a couple miles of driving past more flat-roofed buildings, many of them squashed together along the sidewalk like green chiles in a can, the road dumped me onto the historic plaza downtown.

Its benches, trees, and central monument gave the plaza the aura of an old-fashioned town square somewhere in the Midwest. But only for the first moment or so.

"No Estacionarse," admonished a sign in Spanish. No Parking. From somewhere a few blocks away came the faint sound of a mariachi band. Closer by, I caught a whiff of beef fajitas broiling over an open flame. Two slender, trim old men, wearing thin mustaches, white shirts, and black hats, crossed in front of my car, talking in an archaic dialect of Spanish.

Beneath the shaded walkway of the Palace of the Governors, along

Nasturtiums bloom in an old wagon in the Sena Plaza courtyard. Spanish colonists built on this site in the 1700s and may have lived here before the Pueblo Revolt of 1680, too.

the north side of the plaza, Indian vendors sat in the warm July air with their backs against the cool adobe wall. In front of them black pots, red clay bowls, turquoise necklaces, silver bracelets, sand paintings, and round loaves of bread covered white sheets and Indian blankets.

Yes, this was it, all right. Santa Fe, the city at the end of the trail, my new home.

That was twelve years ago. Since then, I've traveled on writing assignments to Europe and South America and around the United States from Maine to California. But every time I return home to Santa Fe, I feel like kissing the ground. Nothing I've seen on any of my travels can compare to the place that advertises itself as The City Different.

Even so, that first impression still holds: Santa Fe doesn't really exist, at least not in the form in which it has been burbled about and warbled over in more than three thousand newspaper and magazine articles during the past decade. Like a famous actress who lets her fans know just enough about her to intensify her mystique, Santa Fe has concealed as much as she has revealed.

That leads to misunderstandings. Recently I overheard a tourist protest to his wife, "This is Santa Fe? It's nothing like I expected."

So what do people expect?

They expect the qualities they've read about, the basic ingredients of the Santa Fe mystique: The bluest, clearest skies imaginable, and rainbow-colored sunsets. The most intriguing blend of Spanish, Anglo, and Indian cultures in history. Adobe-style architecture with lines so soft that they soothe onlookers into a trance. An arts community like no other. A convoluted colonial history that began before the Pilgrims landed at Plymouth Rock. Sensory pleasures like the aroma of piñon in fireplaces, the taste of *posole,* and the throb of Indian drums. And a gaudy eccentricity in the way Santa Feans see themselves and their city.

That's what people expect, but is it what they get?

Yes and no. The components of the Santa Fe mystique are real enough, but often only in unexpected ways. Mystique, after all, transmutes reality into myth.

In text and photos, this book offers Santa Feans and visitors a taste of the Santa Fe they expect—and the Santa Fe they don't expect.

Autumn foliage conceals all but the tallest buildings and adds to Santa Fe's romantic appeal. For centuries outsiders and residents have argued about what constitutes the reality of Santa Fe. On October 28, 1605, Spanish colonial viceroy Marqués de Montesclaros wrote in a letter to King Felipe III of Spain, "I cannot help but inform your majesty that this conquest is becoming a fairy tale." Even history books have contributed to the myths. In The Modern Part of an Universal History, *published in London in 1763, the authors claimed, "New Mexico extends a great way towards the North Pole."*

Of Palaces And Kings: Downtown and the Plaza

One warm summer afternoon several years ago an acquaintance and I sat on the plaza watching some of the 1.4 million tourists who visit Santa Fe each year. My acquaintance, let's call him Sósimo Apodaca, traces his roots to the first European travelers in the Southwest.

"They say Santa Fe is the oldest capital city in the United States," Sósimo groused in singsong English. Like most Hispanic Santa Feans, he prefers to call himself Spanish and sometimes wears a T-shirt admonishing, "Don't call me Hispanic."

"Well, it is, isn't it?" I asked.

"It's the oldest *occupied* capital city in the United States," he answered. His brown eyes glowed, and he stroked his dark moustache. Passing tourists in shorts and summer dresses pointed to the Palace of the Governors and studied their maps.

I knew what Sósimo meant, but I teased, "Of course it's occupied. People live here. It's not just for tourists."

"No, no. I mean occupied, as in occupied territory. We've got to have a revolution and give New Mexico back to the king of Spain." He laughed and swept his arms outward, startling a fair-haired Swedish tourist. "We'll call it Revolution on the Pecos, or maybe Revolution on Old Pecos Trail."

It sometimes seems as if all 98,000 inhabitants of Santa Fe county have their own version of the city's history. Folk history and recorded history merge and diverge here in ways that amaze both scholars and non-scholars. In other areas of the country, it's impolite to discuss religion or politics. Here the taboo topic is history, which has become a system of belief.

I had read dozens of books on Southwest history and had written numerous history articles and a book on the history of Santa Fe before I understood why. The archaeological and historical records are clear enough and unusual enough to intrigue any curious person. But they are also ambiguous enough, and the issues are laden with enough emotion, to generate endless disagreements and misunderstandings.

Take the question of the city's beginnings.

Between 1860 and 1980, historians and archaeologists found considerable evidence that the ancestors of today's Pueblo Indians lived in what is now downtown Santa Fe long before Spanish explorers arrived in the

The adobe Palace of the Governors on the north side of the plaza remains Santa Fe's most enduring landmark. Early in this century, some scholars claimed to have found the remains of an ancient Indian village beneath the old Spanish government buildings. Others swore that pre-European Indians could have lived anywhere downtown but here. The arguments continue, but historians agree that Pueblo Indians lived in the Palace for thirteen years following the Pueblo Revolt of 1680.

A rainbow over Santa Fe symbolizes the hopes and dreams that have drawn outsiders to Santa Fe since 1821, when the newly independent country of Mexico opened its borders. In the mid-1800s, thousands of Americans traveled from Missouri along the Santa Fe Trail. Today the Santa Fe Trail has become a metaphor for all the different pathways that bring people to the City at the End of the Trail. When French writer Simone de Beauvoir visited Santa Fe in 1947, she wrote in her diary, "After New York and Chicago, after Los Angeles and San Francisco, one feels transported to a magical land."

1500s. Thousands of ancient potsherds emerged from the dirt, and scholars reported the remains of walls and floors of pre-Spanish Indian buildings at several downtown sites, including City Hall, Fort Marcy Hill, and San Miguel Chapel.

Few scholars today dispute the existence of one or more ancient pueblos somewhere in downtown Santa Fe. Somewhere near where tourists now walk, dark-haired, dark-skinned women once knelt to grind their corn with stone *mano* and *metate* (mortar and pestle).

But scholars argue endlessly about the details:

▲ Did ancient Indian settlements at Santa Fe center on the plaza, or a block or so north of that, or elsewhere downtown?

▲ Was this a tiny village, with a handful of inhabitants, a large pueblo, with two thousand or more residents, or something in between? Did its size vary from era to era? Was it several villages clustered together?

▲ Which branch of Pueblo Indians lived here? Tewas? Tanos? Or perhaps even Tiwas, Towas, or Keresans?

▲ How long did they stay? Generations? Centuries? A millennium? And why did they abandon their homes, probably about 1425 A.D.?

▲ Did the name Ogapoge, or Kuapoge, the commonly used appellations of that ancient settlement, refer to the village or only to the locality?

For convenience, Santa Fe's long history is often divided into four eras: Indian (prior to 1425), Spanish (1500s to 1821), Mexican (1821 to 1846), and Anglo or American (1846 to present). Like the Indian era, each of the more recent periods generates intense disputes. In fact, some people protest that to divide history into these arbitrary categories is unfair to all involved.

The arguments extend to the very location of the plaza. Has it always been where it is today? Every historian and archaeologist has a different opinion.

Still, much of Santa Fe's personality comes from its history, and much of that history took place downtown. Here, between 1605 and 1610, the long-abandoned Indian village had its second beginning, as the Spanish colonial regional capital, la Villa de Santa Feé. Paseo de Peralta, a street that encircles the downtown area in the shape of a C, owes its name to don Pedro de Peralta, one of several colonial governors who may have founded the city. (Other possible founders include don Juan de Oñate and his son Cristóbal.) It was Peralta who received orders from the viceroy to construct the *casas reales*—what we call the Palace of the Governors—in 1609.

At that time, Spanish colonial Latin America stretched all the way to the tip of South America. Santa Fe was Spain's northernmost colonial outpost, many days of travel away from the nearest colonial settlements farther south. Mexico City, the viceroyal capital, lay 440 leagues (1,200 miles) away. Traders from Santa Fe and what is now Mexico bought and sold each other's wares, but early Santa Feans lived largely cut off from other colonists.

Infrequent visitors from Spain scolded Santa Feans for laziness. Historical records suggest, however, that the colonists led eventful lives. They made love to each other's husbands, wives, and servants. They accused each other of being witches, Jews, or traitors. They testified piously to the agents of the Inquisition. They scratched at their bedbug bites and chewed on pieces of leather when they had nothing else to eat. They even battled an annoying breed of mice that ate the chiles in the fields faster than farmers could harvest them.

Then came the Pueblo Revolt. In August of 1680, the Pueblo Indians drove the Spanish colonists out of New Mexico. Four hundred settlers died, and many of the 2,500 survivors had to walk barefoot all the way to El Paso. Indians moved into the Palace of the Governors, remodeled it into an Indian Pueblo, and destroyed the Spanish archives.

Twelve years later, don Diego de Vargas and his soldiers rode into Santa Fe at 4 A.M. on September 13 to reclaim it for King Carlos II of Spain. Uncertain what to do, the Indians protested but didn't fight. Neither did the Spanish. This first *entrada* (expedition) into New Mexico led to today's myth of the Peaceful Reconquest. But de Vargas still had to go back to the El Paso area for the colonists. When he returned with them on the second *entrada* in December 1693, lances flew and harquebuses roared, and many Indians died.

For the remaining 128 years of the Spanish era, Spanish colonists and Pueblo Indians alternately cooperated and complained about each other. But the Spanish presence was vital to the Pueblos: The Spanish altered the balance of power and saved the Pueblos from banishment or extinction at the hands of more aggressive Indian tribes.

When Mexico achieved independence from Spain in 1821, New Mexico automatically became part of the Republic of Mexico. But one thing hadn't changed: Political and social upheavals continued.

After gaining independence, Mexico opened its long-closed borders, and American traders, artisans, and trappers flocked down the already ancient Santa Fe Trail, a cluster of trails that connected the Mississippi Valley with the far Southwest. The Americans brought a new set of values and perspectives to Santa Fe. Spanish-speaking writers who lived in New Mexico praised these adventurers for their industriousness, but Santa Fe visitor Henry Smith Turner, an American army captain, wrote acidly, "A truthful American is rarely seen here."

Meanwhile, Spanish and Indian New Mexicans rebelled against Mexico in 1837. They decapitated the governor, used his head as a football, and declared New Mexico's independence from Mexico. Soon the revolt collapsed. Later, Texas invaded New Mexico, hoping to annex it. That, too, failed.

Then on August 18, 1846, Brigadier General Stephen Watts Kearny led the Army of the West into the plaza in Santa Fe. He hoisted the U.S.

Just a block off the main plaza downtown, birds sing, trees bloom, and water rises in the fountain at Sena Plaza. Generations of Santa Feans have eaten, strolled, and dreamed in this hidden courtyard. Once part of a large hacienda, the plaza is now surrounded by shops and a popular upscale restaurant, the Casa Sena.

Above: Twilight colors the sky over San Francisco Street on the south side of the plaza. Woolworth's, the last surviving family store on the plaza, evokes earlier decades, when Santa Feans still out-numbered tourists. When Clyde Kluckhohn visited Santa Fe in the 1920s, he wrote, "Before I had gone six blocks up the narrow crooked streets lined with low adobes, I began to doubt that I was in the United States of North America."

Left: In this crumbling painting on a downtown wall, birds sing to the city's patron saint, San Francisco de Asís (St. Francis of Assisi). His legendary ability to talk with animals ties St. Francis both to Pueblo Indian belief systems and to twentieth-century secular beliefs about Santa Fe as a city in harmony with nature.

flag over the Palace of the Governors, fired a thirteen-gun salute, and proclaimed New Mexico U.S. territory. On a hill northeast of the plaza, where bits of centuries-old pottery still protruded from the earth, his soldiers built Fort Marcy.

Although the United States and Mexico eventually signed a treaty ceding New Mexico to the United States, the builders of Fort Marcy constituted an army of occupation. That's why my friend Sósimo called Santa Fe an occupied city. And that's why a friend of his, let's call him Arturo, can't bear to believe that Indians lived in downtown Santa Fe long before the Spanish arrived. If that is true, then perhaps it makes the early Spanish colonists and their descendants—in short, people like Sósimo and Arturo—occupiers, too.

Even non-Hispanic and non-Indian Santa Feans like to grumble about Santa Fe being occupied. But they're referring to more recent invasions. During the 1980s waves of New Yorkers, Texans, and Californians swarmed into Santa Fe, drawn by the Santa Fe mystique. Few stayed. By one estimate, of every eleven people who moved to Santa Fe in that decade, ten left within two years. But the most recent takeover of downtown Santa Fe occurred at the same time, when most of the old-style shoe stores and family clothing stores near the plaza disappeared, and tourist boutiques took their place.

This problem may seem new, but it isn't. By the mid-1920s, Anglo Santa Feans who were newcomers themselves were muttering about the rise in tourist activities and souvenir stores. They resented people who had arrived more recently than they. In 1926 writer Mary Austin protested the proposed establishment of a "cultural colony" in Santa Fe by a group of Dallas women. "Do you want to ruin Santa Fe?" she raged. "Do you want to spoil everything that makes it what it is?"

Chamber of Commerce President Charles E. Doll countered, "It will bring three thousand people here every summer. They are the best people in Texas. Why shouldn't they come?"

Neither Austin nor Doll would recognize their adopted city today. But arguments like theirs continue between those who want to keep Santa Fe the way it is and those who favor growth and change.

Through all the skirmishes and transformations, the plaza has remained the heart of old Santa Fe. Here you can sit on one of the Mexican cast-iron benches near the small stone marker that commemorates the Santa Fe Trail and soak up the atmosphere. Here you can become part of the quintessential Santa Fe process of interpreting the city's present and past in the light of your own background and interests.

Listen to the bells of St. Francis Cathedral, a block east of the plaza, fling their music through the air. Maybe they'll remind you of church bells you've heard in Europe. Or maybe they'll remind you that history is still being made in Santa Fe. In September 1987, for instance, the bells rang for King Juan Carlos I, who became the first Spanish king ever to visit the city.

Or perhaps the bells will set you thinking about the man whose name the cathedral bears. San Francisco de Asís, the city's patron saint, stands in bronze outside city hall, oblivious to the niceties of separation of church and state. In a sense, he serves as a monument to all the Santa Fe customs and themes that have been transformed from being primarily religious to being primarily cultural. He has even become part of the romanticized version of Santa Fe's name: la Villa Real de la Santa Fé de San Francisco de Asís, the Royal City of the Holy Faith of St. Francis of Assisi.

Maybe the bells will remind you of the cathedral's nineteenth-century builder, French-born archbishop Jean Baptiste Lamy, who battled with native New Mexican clergy like Padre Antonio José Martínez. In her famous novel, *Death Comes for the Archbishop,* Willa Cather cast Lamy as the hero and Martínez as the villain, but many New Mexicans insist that in real life the roles were reversed. Villain or hero, Lamy stands as a bronze statue in front of the cathedral today.

Shifting in your plaza bench, you'll see the portal, or covered walkway, of the Palace of the Governors. Its Spanish colonial look suggests an antiquity that is genuine. Some of the Palace's adobe walls probably formed part of the original *casas reales* constructed by Indians for don Pedro de Peralta. But the current portal dates to a major remodeling of the Palace in 1909–1913. No longer the seat of government, the Palace houses one of four Santa Fe museums that are part of the Museum of New Mexico.

The exhibits in the Palace focus on New Mexico's past. One recent display in the small adobe rooms depicted the Civil War in New Mexico, when the Confederate army burst into Santa Fe in March 1862 and raised the Confederate flag. The men in gray couldn't hold the city, though, and within a month they retreated. After the war, Union General Ulysses S. Grant vacationed in Santa Fe. In the Palace's photo archives, which hold more than 500,000 historic photographs, one photo shows the former general sitting on a padded wicker chair. The neatly bearded Grant holds a black top-hat in one hand, and his feet rest on the broad wooden planks of a typical porch of the era: The boards lie directly on the ground.

The Palace is said to be the oldest public building in the United States. But it's not the only downtown edifice from the Spanish era to survive. West of the plaza on Guadalupe Street, the Santuario de Guadalupe probably dates from the 1790s. It is believed to be the oldest shrine in the United States to Our Lady of Guadalupe, one of the most famous figures in Mexican cultural and religious history. Her painted image and earnest face appear in Santa Fe on everything from entryways to car hoods, testifying to the long-standing, though often overlooked, cultural links between Mexico and Santa Fe.

Another downtown church, San Miguel Chapel, bills itself as "the oldest church in the U.S.A." Scholars insist, however, that it's not. They point to San Agustín Church, built before 1629 at Isleta Pueblo south of

Indian vendors register with the Museum of New Mexico for the right to sit year-round beneath the portal, or covered walkway, of the Palace of the Governors. They may sell only items that they and their immediate families have made by hand, and each piece must carry the artisan's name, initials, or maker's mark. As the sun moves up and down the wall, shading vendors in summer and warming them in winter, they speak Tewa, Tiwa, Towa, Keresan, and other Indian languages among themselves, while tourists browse through the pottery, jewelry, sand paintings, and other craft items.

Above left: An eighteen-year-old French architect designed Loretto Chapel in Gothic Revival style for Archbishop Jean Baptiste Lamy. On December 12, 1887, two months before Lamy died, the archbishop dedicated the stone chapel to Our Lady of Light.

Left: When Loretto Chapel was under construction in the 1870s, local carpenters said they couldn't build a stairway to the choir loft because there wasn't enough space. Then a stranger offered to help. Using neither nails nor supports, he created a staircase that wound up to the loft. Then he refused payment for this masterpiece and disappeared. Santa Feans whispered that it was San José himself— the Biblical Joseph—who had designed and built the miraculous circular stairs. While few take the legend literally, it remains an example of Santa Fe's own brand of magical realism.

Right: Santa Feans still argue about French-born Archbishop Jean Baptiste Lamy's place in New Mexico's history, but all give him credit for founding St. Francis Cathedral. Lamy lobbied for the new cathedral for years before he was finally able to lay the cornerstone on Sunday, October 10, 1869. He mistrusted adobe, and insisted the cathedral be built of stone. French architects, Italian stone cutters, and native New Mexicans worked together to build the new cathedral around the adobe walls of the old parish church. Today a bronze statue of Lamy stands in front of the Romanesque Revival cathedral.

Albuquerque, as one example of an older church. Constructed on the site of an earlier church, San Miguel's adobe walls and roof beams date back only to about 1710. Still, as historian John Kessell has observed, "The triumph of enthusiasm over fact is not always a bad thing." The erroneous belief in San Miguel's antiquity helped focus Santa Feans' attention on historic preservation earlier in this century.

The Gothic-style Loretto Chapel adjoining the Inn at Loretto two blocks south of the plaza looks as if it had sprouted wings and flown over from France. And no wonder. Like the cathedral, these stone walls rose during the reign of Archbishop Lamy, who dedicated the finished chapel on December 12, 1887, shortly before his death. An Austrian carpenter probably built Loretto's winding wooden staircase, which twists up to the choir loft without a single nail or external support. Folk history, though, calls its construction a miracle and attributes the staircase to San José, the Biblical carpenter Joseph.

Throughout downtown, bronze plaques designate other sites rich in history, such as Sena Plaza, a hidden courtyard less than a block from the main plaza. In 1697 Captain Diego Arias de Quiros received this land as a reward for aiding don Diego de Vargas with the reconquest of New Mexico. Over the centuries owners and buildings came and went until, by the 1800s, the Sena family had created a thirty-three-room hacienda around a private plaza. Today the remodeled hacienda houses shops and a restaurant.

In the Senas' old courtyard water splashes in a fountain, and Rocky Mountain redbud trees shower their pink blossoms on passersby. As the petals float down, you can sit and daydream about the husbands, wives, children, grandchildren, aunts, uncles, and cousins who ate and slept and fought and loved here long ago.

Just south of the plaza along Palace Avenue lies the Museum of New Mexico's Museum of Fine Arts, which showcases Southwestern artists like Georgia O'Keeffe, William Penhallow Henderson, Jozef Bakos, and Gustave Baumann. The museum dates only to 1917, but it embodies the essence of Santa Fe's long history. Its adobe walls and rounded lines suggest the architecture of the Pueblo Indians. From certain angles the roofline of the belltowers recalls the Moorish influence on the architecture of Spain. The inner patio, portal, and fountain evoke the most luxurious components of Spanish colonial and Mexican life.

Ironically, however, it was Anglo-Americans, the latecomers, who reassembled these elements and gave that assemblage a name. The museum's architect, Isaac Hamilton Rapp, has been credited with creating something as contradictory, elusive, and debatable as Santa Fe's long history: Santa Fe Style.

Above right: Across a narrow colonial lane from San Miguel Chapel sits an adobe building that bills itself "The Oldest House in the U.S." That's hyperbole, scholars say, but the house probably dates at least as far back as the 1700s, and it may include remnants of walls or floors from Santa Fe's pre–Spanish Indian days.

Right: Over the past two centuries, the tower, wall, and roofline of the adobe Santuario de Nuestra Señora de Guadalupe have shifted shapes like the parts of a transformer toy. In the middle of the last century, the tower sat at one corner of a squattish, sprawling building. After that, the tower moved over and took on the look of a New England spire. More recently, the church reclaimed some of its earlier chunkiness and added elements of California mission style.

Above: San Miguel Chapel claims the title "Oldest Church in the United States." It's not, scholars insist, but it could safely call itself the oldest surviving church in Santa Fe. Between March and September of 1710, a work crew of fourteen men laid down 20,000 adobes to form thick walls on the site of an earlier church. An anonymous artist painted and carved the twenty-two-foot-high altar screen in 1798. In a 1955 excavation, archaeologists from the Laboratory of Anthropology discovered the floors of Indian houses dating to about 1300 A.D. beneath the church. They also found a fragment of sixteenth-century chain mail just beneath the modern floor.

Right: The adobe walls, bell towers, vigas, portal, and courtyard of the Museum of Fine Arts evoke all the eras of Santa Fe's history. That's what city promoters hoped for when architect Isaac Hamilton Rapp received the commission to design the museum in 1916. New Mexicans had used such architectural elements for centuries, but with the building of the museum, Rapp became the official creator of Santa Fe Style in architecture.

Adobe, Chicos, and Desert Chic: Santa Fe Style

▼▼▼▼▼▼▼▼▼▼▼▼▼▼▼▼▼▼▼▼▼▼▼▼▼▼

"**D**er neue Santa Fé-Stil," reads the headline on a recent fashion spread in a German women's magazine: *The New Santa Fe Style.* Silver and turquoise rings and bracelets weigh down the model's brown hands. She sits on a hand-woven Navajo saddle blanket dyed red, black, white, and blue.

All routine enough, as Santa Fe Style goes. But then the text concludes with the thought that anyone who really wants to participate in *Santa Fé-Stil* must wear one final essential: *Lederhosen.*

Lederhosen? German leather pants are an obligatory ingredient in Santa Fe Style?

That couldn't have been what city officials had in mind when, in 1912, they decided that the recently coined phrase "Santa Fe Style" might be just what they needed to transform Santa Fe into "the tourist center of the Southwest." In those years, Santa Fe Style referred mainly to architectural components like those Isaac Hamilton Rapp included in his design for the new museum. But like other inventions over the centuries, Santa Fe Style got away from its creators. Today the term has become so elastic and multifaceted that an operational definition might be, "Whatever you can get away with calling it."

To understand Santa Fe, it's useful to consider the diverse elements and dimensions Santa Fe Style is said to encompass.

For some, it begins with the visual poetry of the curving hills and the muted colors of the earth. For others, it starts with a summer ritual in the parking lot of the Santa Fe Opera, overlooking those sensuous hills. Before entering the open-air opera house to hear world-class singers perform *La Traviata* or *Die Fledermaus,* opening-nighters in tuxedos, formal gowns, and exotic costumes dine on caviar and champagne picnics laid out on tailgates.

For a few, Santa Fe Style means no more than smoking an additive-free brand of tobacco, American Spirit cigarettes, produced by a Santa Fe company. Or it means treating illnesses as varied as head colds and diabetes with herbs like *oshá* and *chamisa hedionda,* which traditional lay medical practitioners called *curanderas* dispense.

For others, the style has to do with religion. For example, in Easter-week pilgrimages, hundreds of Santa Feans of all faiths move one blistered foot in front of the other as they walk the twenty-five miles to a small adobe

Each person has a different definition of where Santa Fe Style should begin and end. "Enough already," shout traditionalists when painted cow skulls and derivative rugs creep into Santa Fe Style.

27

Santa Feans sometimes call The Pink Adobe, a popular Santa Fe restaurant on Old Santa Fe Trail, simply "The Pink." The heavy wooden door, upper-story ladder, window lintels, and flat roof contribute to its Santa Fe look.

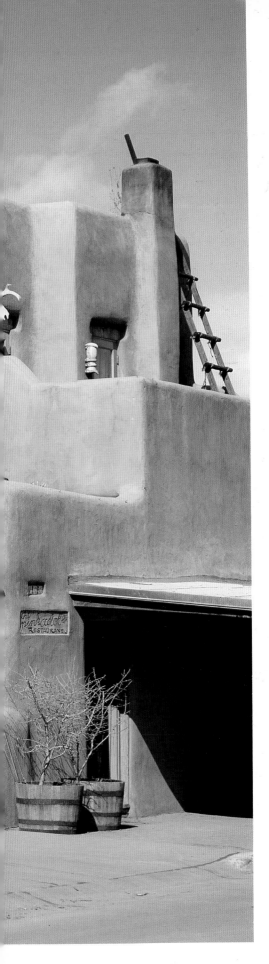

chapel, the Santuario de Chimayó. There they reach into a hole in the floor to grab a handful of dirt that is said to possess healing powers. Meanwhile, *Los Hermanos,* the Penitentes, a centuries-old Catholic lay brotherhood, reenact the Crucifixion at hidden sites outside of town.

For some, true Santa Fe Style died long ago, and what remains is, as an anonymous handbill recently proclaimed, "an insidious illness brought to us by people from Newport Beach, Aspen, Greenwich, and Sausalito." To others, Santa Fe Style is reflected best in these very outsiders, particularly when they bear names like Steven Spielberg and Amy Irving, who married here; or Jessica Lange and Sam Shepard, whose daughter was born at Santa Fe's St. Vincent Hospital.

For others, Santa Fe Style is the almost mystical blending of three cultures—Anglo, Hispanic, and Indian. Opponents counter that it's no more mystical than anything else in life. And anyway, they add, it's not three cultures, but many: Navajo, Pueblo, Spanish, Mexican, and all the European and non-European groups, from Czechs and Afghans to African Americans and Japanese, who wear the catch-all name of Anglos here.

Some maintain that Santa Fe Style is what distinguishes Santa Fe from other tourist towns around the Southwest.

"What does make Santa Fe different from, say, Ruidoso?" I polled a few locals. Ruidoso is a southern New Mexico town popular with tourists.

"Why, the fact that the more fashionable a Santa Fe street is, the less likely it is to be paved," one said.

"Oh, you know, state government," another replied. "That's what makes us different. We have all these government employees, and they don't."

For those who aren't independently wealthy and can't or won't get a job with the state, Santa Fe Style can mean Ph.D.s working as waitresses and former executives driving cabs, even when the rest of the U.S. economy is booming.

Some argue that Santa Fe Style is a misnomer; the correct term is New Mexico Style, Southwest Style, or Desert Chic.

Others say that Santa Fe Style can be illustrated only by anecdotes, all of which conclude with the punchline, "Only in Santa Fe."

Take the case of the tourist I heard call excitedly one day when he saw a crew plastering a Santa Fe wall: "Hey, honey, look! Real adobe!" His wife beamed and turned on the camcorder.

I didn't have the heart to tell them the muddy-looking brown plaster was cement.

Only in Santa Fe.

Or consider the solitary poet, who protests societal definitions of male and female through his attire. He wears a thick beard, clunky hiking boots, and delicate evening gowns. One day a visiting musician from Ecuador, who himself contributed to Santa Fe Style by playing an Andean flute on the sidewalk of San Francisco Street, watched this living symbol of individuality tramp across the plaza.

Asked the Ecuadoran, "Is he some kind of priest?"

Only in Santa Fe.

In short, Santa Fe Style can be construed to relate to any dimension of life. But behind the anecdotes and arias, beyond the dirt lanes and herbs, a few themes recur. This is particularly true in architecture, food, and clothing.

Applied to architecture, the term refers to specific elements that together say Santa Fe. The first is adobe. For centuries the poor mixed straw into clay-rich mud and let the sun dry it into bricks. With these they built their homes. When it rained heavily, houses sometimes dissolved back into mud.

Today only affluent buyers can afford to build adobe homes, and their adobe bricks may come treated with asphalt to prevent water damage. Covered with plaster, these upscale dwellings display fluid lines and soft corners.

Far more Santa Feans live in homes that merely look like adobe. Cover an ordinary wood-frame house with earth-colored stucco, round the corners, add a flat roof, and presto, you have an adobe-style home. Per capita, Santa Fe has more adobe and adobe-look homes than any other city in the country, earning it the unofficial title of Adobe Capital of the U.S.

Generally lumped together under such headings as Pueblo Style, Pueblo Revival, or Pueblo Spanish Revival Style, such homes sometimes show traces of a distinctive variation of Santa Fe architecture: Territorial Style. One of its most obvious distinguishing features is the red brick coping that runs along the perimeter of the roof.

As the name suggests, Pueblo Style borrows features from Pueblo Indian architecture. These include *vigas* (roof beams) and *latillas* (ceiling boards). Originally made of unplaned pine logs, *vigas* may be round or square. Typically they protrude through the walls to the outside. In fact, in adobe-look homes in neighborhoods like Casa Solana, often the only *vigas* are a few ornamental exterior stubs. But these pseudo-*vigas* cast shadows that mark the passing of the seasons and hours just like real *vigas* do.

Latillas, either round or flat, rest on top of *vigas* and originally held up the earthen roof. No matter how close together the *latillas* lay, dirt dribbled through them, so Spanish colonial housewives tacked cloth below the ceiling to catch the falling debris.

To keep their dirt floors dustfree, colonial women hardened and polished them with ox blood. Today, *saltillo* tiles from Mexico and red bricks have replaced blood-firmed earth.

As you enter a typical Santa Fe Style house, you'll see Navajo rugs scattered across these tiles or bricks. Pueblo pots, Hopi Kachina dolls, or Catholic saint figures sit in the *nichos* (display nooks inset in the walls). Painted wooden snakes may rest on built-in adobe *bancos* (benches), or bandanna-sporting coyotes may stand among the ornately carved or boldly plain

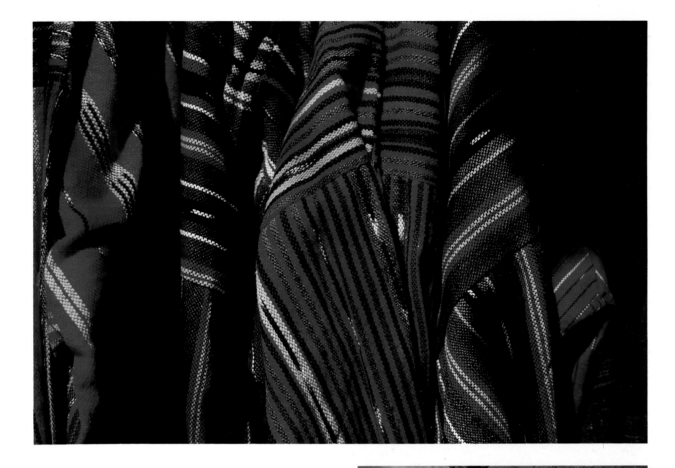

Above: Santa Fe Style clothing ranges from the flamboyant to the conservative. Fabrics from Guatemala and Mexico reflect the fashion influence of Latin America.

Right: A Spanish-speaking woman of northern New Mexico uses a long-handled wooden spatula to take bread out of a beehive-shaped adobe horno *(oven) at Rancho de las Golondrinas. Without thermometers or heat gauges, Spanish and Indian women of New Mexico have baked in these outdoor ovens for centuries. Today bread baked in* hornos *is called oven bread to distinguish it from another longstanding New Mexico treat, fry bread.*

31

As the decorator admits, this living room could be subtitled Santa Fe Baroque. Pueblo pots and Navajo sand paintings stand on the mantel. A cow skull and chile posters hang on the wall, and a Navajo saddle blanket lies on the floor. Ojos de Dios in front of the kiva fireplace and on the wall reflect an old New Mexico custom of guarding a home against the Evil Eye. True to the eclectic spirit of Santa Fe Style, other furnishings come from Oriental and South American traditions.

wooden furniture. Where two walls join, piñon logs burn in the rounded corner fireplace and throw off almost as much warmth as a wood stove. Your host might even serve fresh bread he or she has baked outdoors in a beehive-shaped adobe oven, the *horno*.

The city has an official policy of preserving Santa Fe Style in architecture. The goal is to keep Santa Fe's architecture distinctive from that of other cities but consistent and historically correct within the heart of old Santa Fe. To that end, about 20 percent of the city, including downtown and most of the central east side, has been assigned to one of five local historic districts. When homeowners and businesspeople in these areas restore, remodel, or even do ordinary maintenance, they must follow ordinances that dictate everything from the color of exterior paint to the use of signs.

Codes vary from district to district, but they are strictly enforced. In 1988, when the new owner of the Original Trading Post on San Francisco Street repainted the wooden facade of his curio store bluish gray to give it a weathered look, the Historic Design Review Board ordered him to restore it to the original black. In 1991, when a homeowner installed a painted, bull-shaped gate at his eastside home on Camino del Monte Sol, the board instructed him to remove the nontraditional gate, and the city council concurred. In coffee shops and on street corners, Santa Feans argued about the virtues of sameness versus diversity. As the caption of a newspaper cartoon put it, "Why do they call it 'The City Different'? It all looks the same to me."

Isaac Hamilton Rapp may have created Santa Fe Style in architecture, but his successor, John Gaw Meem, expanded and popularized it during the 1920s, 1930s, and later. Among Meem's many Santa Fe commissions, he designed the Museum of New Mexico's Laboratory of Anthropology, just off Old Santa Fe Trail. He remodeled La Fonda, a hotel on the plaza originally designed by Rapp. And he designed Cristo Rey Church at the lower end of Upper Canyon Road.

Today architects worldwide use elements pioneered by Rapp and Meem and call the results Santa Fe Style, sometimes to the astonishment of Santa Feans. For a time in the early 1990s, buildings that were being constructed outside Paris, France, as part of the new Euro Disney complex of hotels produced a clamor among Santa Feans. When they saw pictures of the stark, still-unfinished hotel, a chorus of Santa Feans protested, "It's not true Santa Fe Style." But others suggested that the zigzagging roofline and proposed decor, right down to an artfully erupting volcano and a sculpture of a flying saucer, simply represented a natural evolution of Santa Fe Style.

Ah, Santa Fe.

In foods, the evolution from style to Style is, in some ways, even more pronounced. Early American travelers found Spanish Santa Feans dining on tortillas, beans, chile peppers, chocolate, *posole* (hominy stew), and *atole,* a thin cornmeal gruel. But the single most fundamental food item, wrote trader and historian Josiah Gregg in 1844, was chile peppers. Red chile "enters into nearly every dish at every meal, and often so predominates as entirely to conceal the character of the viands." New Mexicans ground it into sauce and used it "even more abundantly than butter." They ate the equally fiery green chiles as salads.

Today menus at most of Santa Fe's more than two hundred restaurants omit *atole*, although you can sip it at such functional establishments as the Realburger on Don Gaspar. But tortillas, beans, and, above all, chile peppers (which, as purists like to point out, are not truly peppers at all) abound.

For some chefs and recipe inventors, the basic rule seems to be, the more piquant the dish, the better. That approach sometimes sends visitors scurrying back to good old meat and potatoes. Other chefs use chiles less lavishly or cook with blander, eater-friendly varieties. Either way, many dishes in the gaggle of cookbooks on Southwest cuisine and at fashionable upscale Santa Fe restaurants like Coyote Café, Santacafé, and Casa Sena make *posole* look passé. Try munching some Ancho-Walnut Cream Tea Sandwiches. Or how about White Truffle Tamales, Red Chile Pesto Clams, Sichuan Chicken Fajitas, or Salmon Burritos?

Do such dishes merit the label Santa Fe Style? According to that operational definition of Santa Fe Style as "whatever you can get away with," then, yes, absolutely. Mango Raspberry Brulée is definitely Santa Fe Style. So is Avocado Cake with Blue and Gold Tortilla Arrows. Chefs and restaurants, not just in Santa Fe but from Washington State to Maine and from London to Italy, do get away with calling such dishes Santa Fe Style. Whether that's right or wrong, good or bad—indeed, whether you decide the food is tasty or unpalatable—depends as much on the metaphorical tastebuds in your heart as those in your mouth.

Some longtime Santa Feans wouldn't feed such fare to a goat. When I asked a prominent local writer whose family has lived in New Mexico for centuries what he thought of Santa Fe Style foods, his answer was unprintable. Between the Spanish, Indian, and English expletives, I did catch the recurring phrase, "cultural exploitation."

I've sampled this nouvelle cuisine often enough to learn that sometimes it tastes like a kindergartner's experiments, but other times it's genuinely savory. Still, my own first choice remains such fare as *chico* stew, a meat-and-corn dish that forms a basic part of Pueblo Indian feasts. Or plain old-fashioned masa-and-pork tamales. Or *sopaipillas,* those puffy pieces of fried bread dough which migrated to New Mexico from Chihuahua, Mexico. Or *sopaipillas'* offspring, Indian fry bread. Both hold more grams of fat than most eaters may care to know, but they taste so good that few mind.

And you haven't really eaten until you've sampled *piki* bread. Indian women prepare this gauze-thin tortilla by heating a flat stone in a fire. Meanwhile, they stir water that has been soaked in ashes into blue cornmeal.

Above right: Some of the adobe walls of El Zaguan, an old hacienda on Canyon Road, reach four feet thick. The painted window shutters reflect ancient beliefs. In pre-colonial times, some Indian tribes considered turquoise and other shades of blue sacred, capable of guarding them against evil. After the Spanish arrived, blue began to represent the Virgin Mary, and colonists painted their windows and doors blue to keep evil from entering a house. For most Santa Feans today, blue is just blue, but various shades of turquoise, blue, and aquamarine still appear on windows, gates, fences, and doors around town. Cynics say the hue still wards off evil: the evil of not fitting in.

Right: For two decades New Mexico native Betty Stewart has designed and built traditional Santa Fe Style homes. "Real Santa Fe Style is relaxing," she says. "It should give you a sense of something solid." This corner, in a passageway off Stewart's living room, illustrates her fondness for simplicity and for such traditional elements as tin light covers, hand-hewn wooden doors, old-fashioned locks, and thick adobe walls.

35

Above: Many regard Mark Miller's Coyote Café as the originator of nouvelle Santa Fe Style foods. In this simple dish at the Coyote Café, blue-corn enchiladas in a green-chile sauce prove the connection between new Santa Fe foods and old.

Left: Chile peppers provide the single most important flavor in Santa Fe Style cuisine. Explorer Antonio de Espejo brought chiles to New Mexico in the 1580s, and for centuries Santa Feans have strung red chiles into elongated garlands known as ristras. *When a meal needs more spice, the cook twists off a chile and pops it into the pot. These days, though, most people hang up* ristras *simply to beautify their homes.*

Then they grease the stone with sheep's brain and spread the thin cornmeal batter onto the stone.

Or try shaking a piñon tree with pitch-covered hands to harvest the nuts, as Spanish and Indian Santa Feans have done for centuries. Now that's Santa Fe Style. Or, some autumn day, string red chiles into a long strand called a *ristra*, then pluck them one by one to add to stews all winter, just as local people have for generations. (Don't try that with store-bought *ristras*, though. Most have been shellacked.)

Then there's Santa Fe Style in clothing. Back in the 1830s, according to Gregg, men wore low-crowned, wide-brimmed hats, cloth jackets embroidered with braid, and riding chaps ornamented with filigree buttons and tinsel lace. Sashes, leggings, garters, and ponchos completed the outfit.

Women wore loose white blouses, colorful full skirts, and shawls. They also loaded their bare necks, arms, and fingers with jewelry. Gregg, accustomed to restrictive, concealing dresses in the United States, found Santa Fe women's fashions "a very graceful sort of undress."

A woman attired that way today, right down to the abundant jewelry, would be recognized instantly for her Santa Fe Style. So would someone wearing geometric Indian designs, Navajo ribbon shirts, velveteen full skirts and overblouses, some styles of moccasins, and maybe even buckskin jackets. But much of what passes as Santa Fe Style, including certain brands of slacks—not to mention *Lederhosen*—surprises Santa Feans. We tend to dress eclectically, informally, colorfully, and, yes, eccentrically. But no matter how people elsewhere define Santa Fe Style, that's usually not what Santa Feans themselves are wearing.

In the end, perhaps Santa Fe Style is best summed up by those who make light-hearted fun of it. Take artist Jerome Milord, who, like other artists, contributes an essential ingredient of Santa Fe Style: its arts and crafts. In his classic poster, Milord portrays a living room. A fire burns in the kiva fireplace. In front of a tiled *banco*, an ornamental coyote howls at the *vigas* and *latillas*. A *ristra*, a cowskull, and other Desert Chic trappings hang on the wall. A Navajo rug accents the brick floor. On the rug a woman lies face up, unconscious. She wears silver and turquoise jewelry, and a big silver concha belt cinches down her full skirt and overblouse.

Reads the caption, "Another Victim of Santa Fe Style."

Above left: Outside a shop on Guadalupe Street, Santa Fe Style furnishings absorb the June sun. In Spanish colonial days, Santa Fe Style in rugs meant black-and-white twill carpets known as jergas.

Left: Adobe lends itself to still-lifes, as this simple composition of an old broom, milk can, and enamel coffee pot show. Arranged against an adobe wall, they suggest the slower pace of life in Santa Fe in former days.

Overleaf: Curving lines and flat roofs give these homes off Hyde Park Road a Santa Fe Style look even at a distance. When Zebulon Pike visited Santa Fe early in the 1800s, he wrote, "Its appearance from a distance struck my mind with the same effect as a fleet of the flat bottomed boats which are seen in the spring and fall seasons descending the Ohio River."

Above: When Americans first traveled to Santa Fe in the 1800s, they discovered that Santa Fe Style in eating meant drinking beverages after, not during, a meal, and using one's knees as a dining table. Today, as then, Santa Fe Style in dining includes not just the foods, but the ambience. At La Plazuela restaurant at La Fonda (a hotel on the plaza), stone floors, turquoise tablecloths, diffuse natural light, and hanging plants help give diners that certain Santa Fe feeling.

Left: Santa Fe Style in architecture grew out of earlier centuries' simple building techniques. By 1917 Santa Fe artist Carlos Vierra could accurately prophesy, "We are to be in the future what we build today." The contemporary residence pictured here features the vigas, *curved lines, window lintels, and staggered roofline typical of Santa Fe Style.*

From Fine Art
to Fine Junk:
Arts and Crafts

▼▼▼▼▼▼▼▼▼▼▼▼▼▼▼▼▼▼▼▼▼▼▼▼▼▼

If you drive southwest from Santa Fe along Interstate 25, in a few miles you'll reach La Bajada, a hill that for centuries has led travelers off a saucerlike mesa and into the Río Grande valley. At the foot of La Bajada, a billboard demands, "Messrs. Picasso, Monet, van Gogh: Please step aside for Thomas S. Macaione, the new star in the art world firmament. Let him bask in the light of world fame."

The history of the arts in Santa Fe goes so far back that no one can say when it began. Still, we have a fair idea about the past one thousand years and the influence of each succeeding cultural wave on the city's arts today.

A thousand years ago, Santa Fe Indians dipped yucca brushes into clay-based paints and drew zigzag lines on their clay pots. Today, contemporary pots in Santa Fe galleries bear some of the same designs.

Seven hundred years ago or so, when nomadic Athabascans—today's Navajos and Apaches—drifted in from the north, they learned from the Pueblo Indians how to weave yucca fibers and cotton. Later they acquired sheep and goats from the Spanish. Today, geometrically patterned Navajo wools are better known than either Pueblo or Spanish weavings.

Almost as soon as the Spanish settled in Santa Fe, the city began to develop as a center of the arts and crafts. When artisans in the village's workshops painted animal hides, they probably came the closest to today's definitions of fine art. Spanish colonists and the Indians who worked for them practiced a dozen or more folk arts, too. They whittled cottonwood stumps into three-dimensional images of saints, known as *bultos,* and painted flat saint figures known as *retablos.* (Collectively, *bultos* and *retablos* are called *santos.*) They adzed out a whole line of folk furniture, including storage hutches called *trasteros.* When they could, they worked silver and gold. Otherwise, they applied intricate designs to wood using "poor man's gold" — bits of straw. Later, when it became available, they punched, pressed, and painted "poor man's silver" —tin—to form everything from picture frames to candle holders. After declining during the early part of the American era, these arts thrive again today.

The Mexican influence, subdued but real, throbs with the music of the mariachi bands. It whirls with the colored skirts of the Ballet Folklorico

Since the 1700s or earlier, Spanish and Indian folk artists of New Mexico have painted flat and three-dimensional images of Mexican religious figure Nuestra Señora de Guadalupe—Our Lady of Guadalupe. Her symbolism extends to the secular. Politically, she stands for the triumph of the weak over the strong. In terms of humanistic psychology, she stands for the power of persistence and love. In a social context, she represents equality and acceptance for all. And in feminist terms, she symbolizes the power of women. Here, noted Santa Fe santera Marie Romero Cash gives this Guadalupe figure a New Mexican Spanish look.

dancers, and it stares out of Rivera-esque and Orozco-esque murals around town.

When the Anglos, that most ethnically varying group of all, arrived, they brought a strong emphasis on the fine arts. They also contributed salesmanship, enthusiasm, and hyperbole—both regarding their own art (witness the La Bajarda billboard) and regarding the mountains, hills, villages, and people they encountered. By the mid-1800s, the special, glowing northern New Mexico light and intensely blue skies had begun to intrigue passing artists from as far away as Germany. Gradually other artists followed and stayed.

In 1878, when Indiana-born writer-artist Lew Wallace arrived in New Mexico to assume command as territorial governor, he wrote home to his wife Susan, "What perfection of air and sunlight! And what a landscape I discovered to show you when you come—a picture to make the fame of an artist, could he only paint it on canvas as it is."

In 1893, writer Charles Lummis enthused, "Under that ineffable alchemy of the sky, mud turns ethereal, and the desert is a revelation. It is Egypt, with every rock a sphinx, every peak a pyramid."

But perhaps world-renowned writer and painter D. H. Lawrence expressed the mood and tone of the artistic response best when he wrote in a 1931 essay, "The moment I saw the brilliant, proud morning shine high up over the deserts of Santa Fe, something stood still in my soul, and I started to attend."

What artist wouldn't want to head for Santa Fe after reading testimonials like that?

Several thousand painters, sculptors, writers, musicians, photographers, and other artists live in Santa Fe now, and it is believed that, per capita, the former Villa de Santa Feé has more artists than any other major city on earth. Art galleries have blossomed like wildflowers after a spring downpour, and Santa Fe is said to be the third largest arts center in the United States, after New York and San Francisco.

Some Santa Fe artists sculpt mud with their hands. Others paint curving or geometric abstracts. Some fill canvases with such neo-Romantic symbols of Southwest living as red hollyhocks, adobe walls, canyons, Indians, and cactus. Others, like Apache artist Allan Houser, transform alabaster into Indian figures. Some create art that teases the heart and eye. Dick Mason, for instance, paints New Mexico landscapes in which the juniper-covered hills transmute into dalmations.

Many artists work in several media. Two-time Pulitzer Prize winner Bill Mauldin, a longtime Santa Fean, writes some of the most entertaining books you'll ever read, draws controversial political cartoons, and, in his spare time, transforms his classic Willie and Joe cartoons from World War II into bronze sculptures.

No one artist can typify all the artists in a community. Still, Tommy

At the gallery of Al Luckett, Jr., on Canyon Road, the oldest parts of the building date to about 1760, and an old-fashioned mud-and-straw plaster covers the adobe walls. Spanish colonial furnishings and carved wooden Christ figures fill the rooms. On the wall shown here, from left to right, hang Agnes Sims's "Corn Dance Ceremony," Peter Hurd's "The Irrigator," and Elizabeth Hanson's "Santo Domingo Corn Dance."

Above: Artists Carlos Cervantes, Carlos Leyba, and Samuel Leyba painted this mural along the Santa Fe River. The title, "Las Tres Culturas del Mestizo" (the Three Cultures of the Mestizo), refers to Spanish, Indians, and their mestizo offspring, La Raza. The Mexican flag forms the shirt of the three-headed figure. The Spanish inscription suggests gloomily that New Mexico was "born to suffer and to be exploited by natives, colonists, friends, and enemies."

Left: He may have been Italian, but St. Francis sports a Spanish beard in these carvings by contemporary santero Felix Lopez. In Santa Fe, two streets have been named in the saint's honor: St. Francis Drive and San Francisco Street.

Right: Along with artists and galleries, art collectors complete the triad that makes up the Santa Fe art scene. Santa Fe folk art specialists Chuck and Jan Rosenak collected these Navajo figures by Navajo folk artist Johnson Antonio. Antonio carves his men, women, children, dogs, and sheep from cottonwood. Then he paints them with watercolors and a ceremonial painting clay called dleesh.

Macaione, of billboard renown, has been said to epitomize Santa Fe art. At the very least, his life reveals much about the Santa Fe art scene. Born in New London, Connecticut, in 1907, he studied art briefly in Rhode Island and New York, worked as a barber, and traveled in Europe before moving to Santa Fe in the early 1950s.

The big names in Santa Fe art when Macaione arrived included German-born Gustave Baumann and French-influenced Randall Davey. Three of the five "Cinco Pintores" (five artists) group of the 1920s and 1930s—Josef Bakos, Fremont Ellis, and Will Shuster—still lived and painted in Santa Fe. By then, they'd become so well known that they no longer had to rent out their houses to tourists in the summer to support their art.

Macaione did what newcomers often do. He set up his easel on the streets and began painting Santa Fe's adobe walls, cottonwoods, sunflowers, and lilacs. A dashing man with curly dark hair and a thick mustache, he encouraged people not to twist their tongues trying to pronounce his name. "Just call me Tommy Macaroni." Soon he was being dubbed "The Sixth of the Cinco Pintores" and even "El Diferente" as a tribute to his affection for the City Different. In 1970 the mayor of Santa Fe proclaimed Tuesday, November 24, 1970, El Diferente Day in Macaione's honor.

Since then, the artist's bushy hair has grown long and white and his debonair black mustache has become a thick white beard. Hundreds of artists have moved here, and some have moved on. But Macaione continues to paint on the streets of Santa Fe. He has been named one of Santa Fe's living treasures. The Museum of Fine Arts mounted a special exhibit of his work, and the Santa Fe *Reporter* designated him Santa Fe's Most Unusual Character and Best Artist for 1991. His detractors complain, however, that he has never become part of the art establishment, and they grumble that for a former barber—even one who cut hair to support his art—he receives more attention than he deserves.

For his part, Macaione ignores both praise and censure. He still prefers to sell directly to buyers rather than in galleries. But paintings he couldn't give away in 1955 now go for as much as $10,000.

He also gets around. One hot afternoon, I was visiting San Xavier del Bac, an eighteenth-century church south of Tucson, Arizona, and there sat El Diferente at work in the dusty parking lot. His arthritic fingers held the brush firmly as he filled the canvas with blue sky and white church walls. "What are you doing so far from Santa Fe?" I asked.

He shrugged, and replied in his friendly, cracking voice, "Oh, you know. Tucson. Santa Fe. After a while it's just all more of the same old thing."

Then the octogenarian flitted on like a summer hummingbird to his favorite topic. "Say, did you hear I'm running for President again?" He stabbed his brush at the air. "I stand for world peace and universal brotherhood. I sure hope you're going to vote for me."

Not all Santa Fe artists are so flamboyant. But like Macaione, most

Above: Once Santa Feans stopped arguing and agreed that this bronze buffalo by artist Dan Ostermiller belonged on its median, an anonymous buyer herded it away. Officially, no one will say where the buffalo roams today. Sightings have been reported as far away as China and as close as a well-hidden Santa Fe back yard.

Right: Artist Bob Haozous titled this steel sculpture outside the Wheelwright Museum "Zen Form V." The son of noted Apache artist Allan Houser, Haozous adopted the Indian spelling of his surname.

Above: Artist Tommy Macaione squints in the May sunshine as he talks to passersby on the plaza about politics, life, and art. To some, Macaione is the quintessential Santa Fe artist. To others, the attention and honors he receives illustrate everything that's wrong with the Santa Fe art scene.

Left: Artist Luis Cogley hunts through junkyards for scrap metal with which to make his popular Southwest kitsch wall hangings and garden pieces. Like other kitsch artists, he plays with stereotyped motifs from Southwest cultures and landscapes.

search for a special niche that will fulfill their artistic yearnings and still earn them a living.

Consider Luis Cogley. Born in South America in 1946, he came to Santa Fe from California in 1989 with five children to support. After trying several other media unsuccessfully, he invented a popular variation on the general theme of Santa Fe kitsch. He scavenges at wrecking yards for hoods, fenders, trunks, and other metal parts of cast-off cars. These he carts to his home in Apache Canyon, just outside Santa Fe. There he cuts, welds, and transforms them into Southwest-style churches, adobe buildings, Madonnas, coyotes, rattlesnakes, giant lizards, and more. Popular with tourists, his recycled art owes something to Picasso, something to the Cinco Pintores—and even more to Toyota, Chevrolet, and Ford.

Or take Marie Romero Cash. When she was growing up in Santa Fe in the 1940s and 1950s, she'd never heard of *bultos* or *retablos*. By then that ancient folk art had retreated to the villages of northern New Mexico.

In the late 1970s, however, Cash discovered the old chapels of northern New Mexico. There she saw carved wooden statues of San Francisco de Asís, San Juan Nepomuceno, Our Lady of Guadalupe, the Santo Niño de Atocha, Our Lady of Sorrows, el Nazareno, and many more.

Soon she was painting altar screens and making her own *bultos* and *retablos*—not from religious devotion, but as an artistic expression, as a way of continuing her cultural heritage. One day, as I watched her brush red paint on three black-bearded Spanish men who represented the Trinity, she summed it up: "I don't want to sound too New Age or anything, but I think at some point in time you're headed toward this particular space in your life, and that's what this comes from."

Her *santos* sell in galleries in Santa Fe and beyond from a few hundred up to several thousand dollars. But she also sells directly to buyers at one of Santa Fe's least publicized but most color-filled annual events, the summer Spanish Market, held on the plaza and in the courtyard of the Palace of the Governors the last full weekend in July.

Most of the best works reflect the same traditional styles, year after year. Even so, I never get tired of Spanish Market. There's something wonderfully soothing about standing in front of the Palace of the Governors surrounded on all sides by these ancient arts. At one table, Angelina Delgado Martínez, the seventyish granddaughter of a noted Santa Fe tinworker, displays her punched and pressed tin mirror frames, chandeliers, and other pieces of utilitarian tin art. At another table, Vicki Rodríguez, also of Santa Fe, holds up a box she has decorated with poor man's gold. Nearby, María Fernández Graves of Ranchos de Taos shows off her *colcha* embroidery, and Eppie Archuleta of Alamosa, Colorado, sells her Río Grande weavings.

Other artisans hawk ornate Spanish furniture, carved wooden trees of life, and cottonwood images of San Francisco de Asís. To ensure that yesterday's folk arts won't disappear, smiling youngsters aged five and up

A totem pole stands outside the Fletcher Gallery on Canyon Road. Housed in a building that dates back to the 1700s, the gallery shows works by such noted local artists as Rudy Fernandez, Jane Shea, and Janet Lippincott.

sell their own attempts at traditional art at tables in the center of the plaza.

At the 1991 Spanish Market, what caught my attention most was a piece that a Los Angeles museum had purchased: a life-sized wooden skeleton of a woman in a wooden cart. "It's Doña Sebastiana," her creator, Nicholas Herrera of El Rito, New Mexico, explained. "La Muerte. Death. She's everywhere, you know." That sense of death in life is an enduring undercurrent in the arts of Santa Fe.

But then, so are drama, foolishness, and conflict. In December 1988, for instance, sculptor Charles Southard's depiction of a life-sized steel burro, loaded with wood, went up at the corner of Sandoval and Water streets beside the city's new parking garage. Nothing wrong with the burro, critics muttered, except that it was too small and the parking garage too large.

Then someone noticed the name: "Homage to the Burro." To Anglo ears, it sounded fine. But to a Spanish member of the Santa Fe Arts Commission, "burro" seemed all wrong. That name applied to stubborn humans, he said; the animal was a *burrito*.

Southard changed the name, and the city arts director mailed out six hundred engraved invitations to the dedication of "Homage to the Burrito."

Then someone else protested that burritos are for eating, not carrying wood. The artist groaned and said he didn't care what name the steel animal wore. In the end, with human burros on all sides grumbling, the critter too was renamed a burro.

Or consider the case of the buffalo and the coffee cup.

Throughout Santa Fe, local businesses volunteer to beautify assigned sections of street medians as part of the Santa Fe Beautiful program. One day early in 1989, someone at Nedra Matteucci's Fenn Galleries on Paseo de Peralta realized that the triangular median the gallery had adopted would be a great place to display a piece of art. The mayor agreed, and in April a crane lowered a six-foot-high, 1,600-pound bronze buffalo among the flowers. Artist Dan Ostermiller had created such a lifelike animal that it appeared ready to eat them.

The buffalo was hardly in place when a city official pronounced it a traffic hazard and a legal liability. "The buffalo will have to be removed," he announced. The city transportation director concurred.

Santa Feans, however, had already fallen in love with the hairy, muscular bronze symbol of the Old West. School children posed in front of it holding a "Save the Buffalo" sign. Citizens called the mayor's office to plead for the beast. Tommy Macaione painted the buffalo for a poster, the proceeds of which would help buy the $45,000 sculpture for the people of Santa Fe.

Finally the city council announced that the buffalo could graze on its median until October 1.

Meanwhile, another Santa Fe business, noting the appeal of the buffalo, placed a six-hundred-pound cup and saucer in its median, and labeled it a bird bath. A new uproar began.

Artworks become part of the scenery in the garden at Nedra Matteucci's Fenn Gallery on Paseo de Peralta. Here, Dan Ostermiller's bronze golden eagle, "American Gold," appears ready to plunge into the water and pluck out a goldfish.

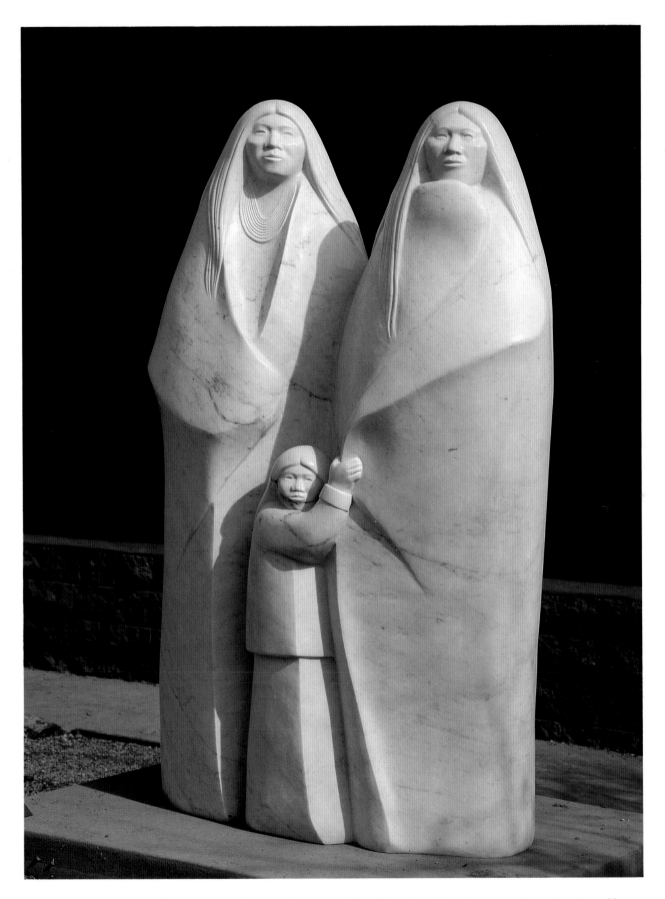

Chiricahua Apache sculptor Allan Houser carved this family grouping, "Here They Come," from Carrara marble. A descendant of famous chief Mangas Coloradas, Houser traces the roots of his art to the stories and songs he heard as a child.

The business in question sold not art, but coffee beans. And the coffee cup was not a highly polished, sophisticated bronze sculpture. It was made of cement.

The mayor was quoted as calling the cup and saucer "un–Santa Fe" and "crappy." Others suggested that as a bird bath it would appeal only to ostriches and flamingos, and they asked, "When was the last time you saw a flamingo in Santa Fe?" The Adopt-A-Median program announced it would cancel the offending business's contract effective October 1, the day the buffalo had to move on.

At the last minute, the city council decided the buffalo could stay, but the coffee cup had to go. A four-foot-tall cardboard tombstone replaced it. The epitaph read, "Here lies freedom of expression, killed by narrow, small-minded intolerance and political manipulations." Then the tombstone, too, disappeared.

And the buffalo? Even El Diferente's poster couldn't raise enough money to save it. An anonymous buyer galloped up to the gallery with cash in hand and lassoed the buffalo away.

There's more to the Santa Fe art scene, of course, like the Museum of International Folk Art. Or the two Indian museums, the Wheelwright Museum of the American Indian and the Museum of Indian Arts and Culture. You can even do arts research at two specialized art libraries.

Santa Fe also overflows with fine writers, like Barbara Beasley Murphy, who includes Southwest themes in her fiction for children and young adults. There are dozens of outstanding musicians, like Elaine M. Grossman, who plays the oboe for the Santa Fe Symphony orchestra. And numerous knowledgeable art collectors, like Chuck and Jan Rosenak, who own a superb collection of Navajo folk art and make their home in the Santa Fe suburbs of Tesuque.

Then there are the art groups, whose members range from the descendants of early Santa Fe artists to artists from Berlin. And of course there are galleries galore, approximately one for every two hundred Santa Feans. One of the most striking is Shidoni, a gallery and foundry in Tesuque. There, each Saturday year-round, visitors watch fiery orange liquid bronze splash into molds. Then they wander out to the sculpture garden, where, surrounded by abstract and realistic art, they enjoy picnics under the apple trees.

Picasso, Monet, and van Gogh probably have nothing to fear. Billboard or not, neither Tommy Macaione nor any other Santa Fe artist is likely to make those giants step aside. But still, Santa Fe wouldn't be Santa Fe without its artists, its art squabbles, and its abundance of art.

Artist Glenna Goodacre's lifelike bronze "Waterbearers" decorates the grounds of the capitol building on the corner of Old Santa Fe Trail and Paseo de Peralta. When the new capitol went up in 1966, people grumbled that it looked like a bull ring, a Roman arena, a Greek temple, or an Indian kiva. However, its design, a circle divided at the circumference into four equal parts, represents a Pueblo Indian symbol, the Zia sun symbol. Theoretically, the Zia binds those who enter—including politicians—to four sacred obligations: a clear mind, a pure spirit, a strong body, and a devotion to the common good. Goodacre's sculptures reflect these themes.

German-born artist Zara Kriegstein, who studied at the Academy of Art in Berlin, designed this mural, "Present Moment," on the side of a building on St. Francis Drive. Created by the Multi-Cultural Mural Group, the tableau depicts the fight against the dragon of oppression and oppressive forces like anger, greed, and gluttony. The violin-playing clown symbolizes serious artists, who make their comments

on life without knowing if anyone listens. The prostitute and the man with the rooster head represent artists and others who have given up their ideals, thereby strengthening the dragon. Says Kriegstein, "Good art will always be controversial." Other painters who worked on this project include Felipe Cabeza de Vaca, Marian Berg, and Susan Contreras.

Corn Mother and Painted Clay: The Pueblos and Beyond

▼▼▼▼▼▼▼▼▼▼▼▼▼▼▼▼▼▼▼▼▼▼▼▼▼

In a large office in Santa Fe, an executive sat answering phone calls, signing letters, making requests to his secretary, and talking to me. I'd seen him before, but I couldn't remember where.

"Oh, you know what they say, all Indians look alike," he said solemnly. I blushed.

"I'm from San Juan Pueblo. Maybe you've seen me dance."

I thought back to the last time I'd visited San Juan, about thirty miles north of Santa Fe. It was June 24, St. John's day, when the people of the village simultaneously celebrate their Catholic patron saint's day and ancient Indian rituals related to crops.

The sun had already taken on its special summer glare. Among the crowd of spectators, the locals stood out from the tourists because most of the New Mexicans wore hats or held umbrellas to protect themselves from that glare. In the big dirt plaza surrounded by mud-plastered adobe houses, a long line of Pueblo men, women, and children raised a haze of dust as they danced. Drums throbbed, and the chanters sang repetitively in a language that I knew must be Tewa, although I could understand none of the words. The women, dressed heavily in blouses, skirts, and shawls in spite of the heat, shuffled in place while the men stomped. Red painted circles that looked like suns gleamed on the women's cheeks.

The men's dress and painted faces varied more. One wore only a breechcloth and yellow moccasins, with yellow streaks on his face, and he shook the rifle in his hand like a rattle. Another, in a white shirt with turquoise polka dots, carried a war shield and wore a headdress of what looked like skunk hair. His face was painted red and blue, in curving lines.

Nearby, under a tree, an old Indian man stood beside his grandson. The little boy tugged at his grandfather's arm. "Grandpa, I forget," he said. "Are we Summer People or Winter People?" The old man lifted the boy into his arms and answered so softly that no one else could hear.

I looked back at the dancers and tasted dust. One man stood out. Over his glistening brown skin he wore an elaborate bead vest. Long strips of what appeared to be fox fur dangled from his feather headband. White paint covered the lower part of his face, and a bell-covered belt jangled at his kilted waist. But what caught my attention was the intent look on

At the Indian Market fashion show, Hopi Wilbert Honahni wears the black-and-white paint of the koshari. In traditional Pueblo beliefs, these clown figures aid in the cure of physical and emotional illnesses. They also entertain the audience during sacred dances.

his face. He seemed engrossed in the chanting, the drum beats, the ritual movements of his arms and hands. For him, none of the hundreds of Indian and non-Indian watchers existed.

I imagined that he was off somewhere in the world of Mother Earth and Father Sky, the world of White Corn Maiden and Blue Corn Woman—a secret ritual world in which people are not just people, but Dry Food People, Made People, and Dry Food People Who No Longer Are. This is the world of the seven directions: north, south, east, west, up, down, and middle; where medicine men each spring open a hole in the Earth Navel, and enter the sacred tunnel to plant the symbolic seed.

Suddenly the businessman's phone rang, dragging me back from San Juan Pueblo to the office in Santa Fe. I looked at him closely as he spoke softly into the mouthpiece. Now I knew. He was the man with the white painted face, sitting before me in a conservative blue suit without beads, feathers, paint, or drum beats.

"It isn't easy," he observed, as he hung up the phone. "In the daytime I'm a typical American businessman. I drive home at night to San Juan, and I'm in a completely different world. My mother's a medicine woman, and she takes her duties seriously." He hesitated, then leaned forward and said, "Did you know that in some of the Keresan Pueblos there are still medicine people who must always be home to the Pueblo by dusk?" Because of their ancient obligation to be present at the Pueblo all night, he explained, they can never travel farther than half a day away from their homes all their lives.

More than 450 years have passed since the first non-Indians arrived in northern New Mexico. Ever since, the Pueblo peoples have had to live with the constant duality between the world views and demands of outsiders and their own traditional perceptions and duties. Many villages have vanished. Nineteen remain. Of these, eight lie north of Santa Fe, and the others lie west and south.

Each Pueblo is politically independent from the others, and the residents of one Pueblo may speak a different language from their closest Pueblo neighbors. North of Santa Fe, the languages are Tewa and Tiwa. South of Santa Fe, the people of Cochiti, Santo Domingo, and San Felipe, for instance, speak Keresan. Other languages include Towa (at Jémez Pueblo) and Zuni (at Zuni Pueblo). Often, to communicate with one another, people from different Pueblos must talk Spanish or English.

For the past hundred years, ever since Anglo artists and writers began romanticizing the Pueblo Indians and their non-Western cosmology, the Pueblos have had to deal almost daily with strangers who idealize them without knowing much about them. For many non-Indians, the Pueblos remain the most powerful and the most exotic of all Santa Fe's allures. The division of all residents of each Pueblo into Summer People and Winter People sounds mysterious to begin with. It seems even more so when you

Costumes and paraphernalia from different tribes illustrate common themes at the Indian Market fashion show. Here, the bear on a hide shield reflects the interconnectedness of human and animal life. Legends of most Southwest tribes include stories of supernatural bears, and the Bear Clan is a powerful group among Pueblo peoples.

realize that this is simultaneously a political, social, and religious division that affects every aspect of life. Add to that the Pueblo belief that the stages of human development fall into categories like Dry Food People and Made People, and it's easy to see why the Pueblos fascinate non-Indians.

"People stare at us as if we were from another planet," complained an Indian acquaintance of mine who still maintains a ceremonial home in the ancient mesa-top village of Acoma, west of Albuquerque. Then she laughed. "They don't seem to realize that they're the weird ones to us."

Renowned Swiss psychiatrist Carl G. Jung learned this himself when he visited New Mexico in 1925. At Taos, the northernmost Pueblo, Jung talked with a tribal leader named Ochwiay Biano, or Mountain Lake.

Together Jung and Mountain Lake stood on the fifth story of one of the oldest apartment buildings in the world. To the east rose the mountains, home of the sacred Blue Lake. To the west the Río Grande gorge sliced the plains. A stream bubbled down from the Blue Lake and through the adobe village, separating it into Summer People and Winter People.

"We think whites are insane," the Indian told his Swiss visitor.

"Why?"

"They say they think with their heads."

Jung looked at him, surprised. "Why, of course. What do you think with?"

The Indian pointed to his heart.

Mountain Lake complained that whites wanted to stamp out traditional Indian ways. "After all," he said, "we are a people who live on the roof of the world; we are the sons of Father Sun, and with our religion we daily help our father go across the sky. We do this not for ourselves, but for the whole world." If the Indians stopped, the sun would cease to rise. "Then it would be night forever."

Dance ceremonies throughout the year are one way the Pueblos work to keep the world in harmony, to keep human beings in balance with nature, and to help the sun move through the sky. Dances and rituals vary from Pueblo to Pueblo, but the basic meanings are the same. When the sun rises on January 23 and an animal figure appears on a hilltop at San Ildefonso Pueblo, it signals not only the beginning of the deer dance but also the interdependence of humankind and animals. When an old medicine man steps out onto the dance plaza at Santa Clara and offers grains of sacred cornmeal on August 12, it signifies not only the start of the corn dance but also the eternal cycle of planting and harvest, spring and fall, summer and winter.

Even the designs on the Pueblos' world-famous pottery tie in with these themes.

Consider award-winning Santa Clara potter Anita Suazo. She and her husband Joseph live in the modern part of the village in a bungalow that looks no different from homes in cities across the United States. He works

Above: A Hopi girl poses in a rainbow headdress at the Sunday morning fashion show at Indian Market. Although they live in Arizona, far from the Río Grande Pueblos, Hopis remain closely linked by culture and religion to their ancestral cousins on the Río Grande. In some cases only a scholar—or a Pueblo Indian—can distinguish Hopi tablita headdresses from those of, say, Santa Clara Pueblo on the Río Grande.

Below left: August's annual Indian Market draws more visitors to Santa Fe than any other event. Market sponsor SWAIA (the Southwestern Association on Indian Affairs) screens participants and requires that they sell only original, handmade arts and crafts of the finest quality. In the opening hours of the two-day market, shoppers and sightseers jam the streets around the plaza.

Below right: At Indian Market a young Zuni woman wears a rainbow tablita headdress as part of the ancient rainbow dance. Like other Pueblo peoples, the Zuni divide the year into Summer and Winter and divide themselves into Summer People and Winter People. The rainbow dance is a summer dance, related to summer thunderstorms and life-giving rain.

all day in Santa Fe; her favorite summer pastime is to attend the Santa Fe Opera. They seldom participate in village ceremonies, but their joint work on her pottery links them closely to traditional Pueblo life.

Each Pueblo makes its own style of pots. Santa Clara is noted for black-on-black, black carved, red carved, and red polychrome pots. Anita Suazo's pots begin with a trip into the countryside, among the juniper trees, mesas, and dry arroyos on Santa Clara tribal land. There, at sites no outsider knows, she and Joseph collect tubfuls of chocolate-colored clay and volcanic ash.

Later, Joseph strains out impurities in the clay and ash and adds water. Then, like an old-fashioned wine maker, he tramps barefoot through the gooey mixture to blend it. As his toes squish in and out, they tell him whether he's added the right amount of ash. Too much, and the pot chips. Too little, and it cracks.

One day when I visited, Anita was making a seed pot. She picked up a clump of brown clay and rolled it back and forth between her hands. A long rope of clay emerged. Carefully she coiled it around and around until she had formed a small pot.

She set that aside and selected another pot in progress, one that had already dried. Then she pulled out a box of water-smoothed river stones. "Every potter collects these," she explained. "We polish the pots with them. Sometimes we use the same stone for years, and with every pot, the stone gets a little smoother." She picked through the rocks until she found a speckled stone with an oblong curve that perfectly fit both her hand and the clay ware. The stone was a gift from her mother, who has been making pots for almost seven decades. Carefully Anita rubbed it across the rough, dry clay.

Another pot, already completed, sat nearby. The elongated red jar was about eight inches high, and she had painted red, blue, and white lines on it using slips of colored clays.

"Here, let me show you how to read those," she said. Soon what had appeared to be abstract designs revealed themselves as mountains, clouds, rain drops, water serpents, lightning, melons, bear paws, and the steps that lead into the sacred ceremonial chamber, the kiva.

Even the shapes of the pottery can have meaning. She picked up a small, earth-toned turtle. Most of her pottery she sells to tourists, but this piece she was saving for a special friend. "Turtles live longer than other animals," she said. "So when we give someone a turtle, it's a way of wishing them long life."

One dimension of Pueblo life doesn't usually show up in their pots, at least those that outsiders see: their humor. Often subtle or oblique, Pueblo humor typically serves to put the world in perspective.

It might, for instance, involve no more than an old cultural figure used in a new context. One cold Christmas day at San Ildefonso Pueblo, I watched men dressed as buffalos perform the ancient buffalo dance. Then another figure emerged from the kiva and moved out to join the herd.

San Ildefonso Pueblo, south of Santa Clara, is noted particularly for its winter dances. On San Ildefonso's feast day, January 23, dancers prance around like elk, deer, and other animals. The ceremony dates to the days when villagers starved if hunters failed to bring home winter game.

He wore turquoise jewelry and carried an Indian prayer stick. Colored beads and fur trimmed his long buckskin gloves. But he also wore a white-face mask to make him look non-Indian. A thick white beard jutted from the mask. He carried a sack over his shoulder and wore a white-trimmed red hat and suit on which jingle bells tinkled. It was Santa Claus, a ritualized, symbol-laden Santa, dancing the buffalo dance.

Or consider an incident that is said to have taken place west of Santa Fe at Jémez Pueblo. One day a woman found out her husband was seeing another woman. The indignant wife slipped a pair of scissors into her pocket and marched off to confront her rival. The wife grabbed the woman by her long, beautiful black hair and snipped it all off.

The tribe didn't interfere. But they reportedly gave the short-haired woman a new name: No Appointment Necessary, or, for short, No Appointment. "Hey, No Appointment, how you doing this morning?"

Another time an editor I worked with assured me that the Pueblo Indians make their *chico* stew with lamb. I thought they used pork. One day when I was visiting the Tapia family at Santa Clara Pueblo, Mrs. Tapia brought a big bowl of *chicos* to the table. Shining yellow corn kernels floated among tender chunks of meat in a peppery broth.

"What kind of meat is this?" I asked, ladling out a bowlful.

Mr. Tapia grinned. "This one's horse." Then he pointed to another bowl, containing *posole*. "And that one's mule."

We all laughed. Months passed before I could confirm that the men and women of Santa Clara usually make their *chico* stew with pork.

In Santa Fe, Pueblo rituals, pottery, dress, and foods come together with those of many other tribes at August's annual two-day Indian Market, when top-ranked Indian artists turn the plaza into an open-air salesroom. Inside the canvas-roofed booths, approximately one thousand Indian artisans lay out $3 million worth of hand-crafted jewelry, pottery, beadwork, sand paintings, sculptures, fetishes, featherwork, baskets, and other traditional and contemporary crafts. But the real crush comes from the buyers, who jam together six and eight deep, waiting for the hands on the old clock on the corner of Palace and Lincoln to reach 8 A.M., the moment when the selling officially begins.

It's the largest single event of the year-round Santa Fe tourist season and the largest market of Indian arts and crafts in the world. Drawing crowds of 70,000 and more from around the United States and abroad, the Indian Market offers buyers authenticated handmade American Indian arts and crafts. One year, a single Navajo rug fetched $60,000. Another year an exquisite concha belt sold for $35,000. But generally prices range from about $2 (for colored corn-kernel necklaces) to $15,000.

Navajo sculptor Larry Yazzie, who works in bronze and in stones like alabaster and marble, is a typical vendor. Born in Arizona in 1958, he graduated with honors from the Institute of American Indian Arts in Santa Fe in 1985

Above: With only slight overlapping from village to village, each Pueblo makes its own styles of pottery. Clockwise from the top, these pieces come from Santo Domingo, Acoma, Santa Clara, Jémez, Tesuque, Santa Clara, and Acoma. Typical Santa Clara designs decorate the pot in the center.

Right: At Indian Market, a Navajo sandpainter sifts colored grains through his fingers to illustrate painting techniques. Properly called "drypaintings" because they include not just sand, but also clay, charcoal, plants, and minerals, these works of temporary art link Navajos to the sacred world of the Holy People—Snake Woman, Monster Slayer, Spider Woman, First Woman, First Man, and others. According to traditional beliefs, the Holy People presented the designs in the paintings to human beings and admonished them to guard the patterns carefully.

Overleaf: The Olla Maidens of Zuni Pueblo create a living rainbow when they line up to perform the traditional olla dance. The first non-Indians to reach Zuni Pueblo, near the Arizona–New Mexico border, in the 1530s, called it Cíbola. When they saw the sun reflecting off the gypsum windows of the six villages of Cíbola, early explorers convinced themselves—and others—that they had found the legendary Seven Cities of Gold.

Pueblo children begin to dance soon after they learn to walk. Their earliest memories include tribal customs and beliefs. Long before they start school, they learn that spruce boughs symbolize long life, gourd rattles imitate the sound of rain falling on crops, and feathers represent the heavens and the zenith of the sky. Here, the children of Santa Clara Pueblo dance.

Each year on August 12 the Tewa-speaking villagers of Santa Clara Pueblo perform ancient dances to ensure a good corn harvest. In a version of the corn dance called the tablita dance, women wear tablitas (painted headboards) decorated with symbols that represent the sky, clouds, sun, moon, corn, and other sacred dimensions of Pueblo life. Even the colors have meanings: Yellow symbolizes pollen, turquoise represents the sky, red signifies blood, and black means death.

and has been selling at the market ever since. Among his many honors and prizes, he received the market's Wheelwright Museum Award for Best New Sculptor/Carver in 1987 and the Best in Division award in 1990.

During one recent Indian Market he stood beside a bronze Indian figure called "Prayer for Mother Earth" and talked about his work. "A lot of my ideas stem from visions and ceremony," he explained. "This one came during an all-night ceremony in which we sing and pray. It's a healing ceremony for all the things that Native American people have problems with."

Another time he sculpted a four-foot chunk of black soapstone into four ascending figures, the healing Yei-bi-cheii dancers. But later a figure in a vision told him the Yeii were too sacred to reproduce in his art, so he decided never to carve another.

Part of the pleasure of Indian Market comes from watching the craft demonstrations. Often, a Navajo woman sits weaving a blanket on a vertical loom on the plaza. One year a Navajo man carefully dribbled colored sands from his hands to create a sand painting. Another year a Pima woman wound willows around cattails and devil's claw to produce a traditional basket. Once a southern Ute woman illustrated beading techniques, and a Chippewa artist sculpted a piece of glistening marble.

In the end, though, it's not tribes who travel from other regions to the Indian Market, like the Chippewa, Ute, or Pima, who best represent Santa Fe. It's the Pueblos, who have breathed the dry air of northern New Mexico for many centuries. It's a woman from Santo Domingo Pueblo who sits selling her family's arts and crafts under the portal of the Palace of the Governors, day after day, in wind, sun, or snow. It's a man who drives to work one morning in a business suit and stomps the earth in a beaded vest the next. It's a little boy sorting out his heritage among the Summer People and Winter People. It's the ability to make jokes about horse meat and mule meat. And it's dark-haired potters like Anita Suazo quietly painting designs on clay as their ancestors did a thousand years ago.

Above: Wearing headdresses and wings, the young people of San Juan Pueblo, north of Santa Fe, perform the eagle dance. As the drummers pound their drums and sing, the dancers imitate the bird's soaring, hovering, perching, resting, and mating rituals.

Below: When the few surviving Pecos Indians abandoned Pecos Pueblo in 1838, they moved to Jémez Pueblo, where people spoke their language, Towa. Today Jémez remains the last surviving Towa Pueblo. To ensure that their language and customs do not die, parents speak Towa with their children and teach them traditional dances. Here, children from Jémez Pueblo perform the butterfly dance on the grounds of the Museum of Indian Arts and Culture in Santa Fe.

When the Spanish arrived in northern New Mexico, they found the Pueblo Indians making clay figurines. For religious reasons, the Spanish tried to force the Indians to stop, but the tradition survived in secret. In the late 1800s, Anglo curio wholesalers discovered that figurines

sold well, and they encouraged potters to make more. Carol Pecos of Jémez Pueblo made the clay storyteller dolls shown here at Indian Market. All storyteller dolls reflect the influence of Cochiti potter Helen Cordero, who made the first known storyteller dolls in 1964.

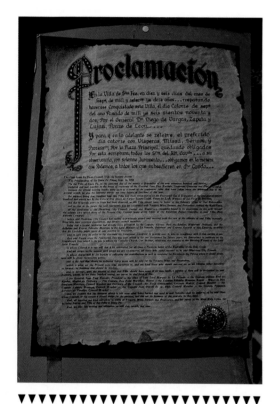

¡Que Vivan Las Fiestas!: Christmas and Other Celebrations

"'**B**urn him! Burn him! Burn him! Burn him!'" chant the 40,000 Santa Feans and visitors who overflow Fort Marcy Park one Friday night each September. Looming over them on a hillside, a forty-six-foot-tall white monster flails his arms, tosses his head from side to side, and moans with unearthly sounds that can be heard all the way to the plaza, a few blocks away. White-robed figures called Glooms surround the monster. A Fire Dancer taunts him with a glowing torch, while fireworks explode all around.

It sounds like some kind of pagan ritual, or a scene from a low-budget horror film. But this, after all, is Santa Fe. Even the festivals have a distinctly Santa Fe quality to them.

Take the Fiesta de Santa Fe. That's Zozobra, an effigy of Old Man Gloom, thrashing around up there on the hillside. When a stray spark finally sets his muslin, paper, and wooden body ablaze, his black eyes turn red. Flames shoot from his lips, and powdery gray ashes float down on the crowd.

But more than Zozobra goes up in smoke. During the 180 seconds it takes to reduce Old Man Gloom to charred chicken wire, folklore asserts that all the sorrows, misfortunes, and stresses Santa Feans have experienced over the past year vanish, too.

"¡Que vivan las fiestas!" People of all ethnic backgrounds call exuberantly as they walk slowly away through the night. *Long live Fiestas!* Others shout more personalized *vivas*. One year a man in front of me bellowed, "¡Que viva Pancho Villa!"

Pancho Villa, long-dead hero of the Mexican Revolution of 1910? What does he have to do with Fiesta?

Absolutely nothing. But that's just the point.

Like art galleries and restaurants, festivals come and go in Santa Fe, but a few endure. These include spring and fall festivals at Rancho de las Golondrinas, special Christmas celebrations, and above all, September's weekend-long Fiesta de Santa Fe.

Fiesta often goes by the long-winded title, "Oldest Ongoing Community Celebration in the United States." (Purists argue whether the correct name is Fiestas or Fiesta; take your pick.) During the first Fiesta, in September 1712, Santa Feans paraded around the plaza to honor the safe return of the Spanish to Santa Fe after the Pueblo Revolt. City officials

On September 16, 1712, city founders proclaimed a new holiday for Santa Fe, to be held each September, "forever." Today their new holiday, now called Fiesta de Santa Fe, or simply Fiesta, has become known as the oldest ongoing community celebration in the United States. This twentieth-century reproduction of the original bando *(decree) includes an English translation.*

announced that this holiday was to be "celebrated forever." But when the Mexican era arrived, more than a century later, Fiesta stopped honoring the Spanish return to New Mexico and started celebrating their expulsion from Mexico instead.

Over the decades the holiday alternately flourished and declined, until Anglo promoters revived it early in this century with pageants, parades, and pomp. Then in 1926 artist Will Shuster, one of the Cinco Pintores, borrowed from effigy-burning traditions in Latin America and Spain to create Santa Fe's first Zozobra. It's been the most popular part of Fiesta ever since.

Through the years, the festival's underlying themes of celebration and commemoration have endured. Some Santa Feans dance in the streets or at formal balls. In the plaza young men and women twirl across a temporary stage in the ritual steps of folk dances from Jalisco, Yucatán, Michoacán, and other Mexican states.

Other Santa Feans pass through the city's narrow streets in religious processions that honor La Conquistadora, a statue of the Virgin Mary that is said to date back to 1626. Still others, for whom La Conquistadora sounds like some kind of female conquistador, line the streets to watch the Hysterical-Historical Parade. Little boys in *charro* (cowboy) costumes grin from beneath ornate sombreros, and shining red *troquitas bajitas*—low-rider trucks—follow the floats.

On Saturday afternoon, performers dressed as Spanish soldiers ride into the plaza to reenact the pageant of *La Entrada,* the peaceful first return of don Diego de Vargas to New Mexico in 1692. Today, as in 1712, this is again the official raison d'être of Fiesta.

Most years, local Indians refuse to participate in this commemoration of their defeat. They ask whether it's appropriate to hold a festival, year after year, that celebrates the triumph of one ethnic group over another. Other critics remind anyone who will listen that the actual return of the Spanish colonists, the second *entrada,* was bloody, not peaceful.

· People nod, smile, and sympathize. But Fiesta and the pageant proceed. The non-Indian Santa Feans chosen to take the Indians' place smear themselves with brown paint, don feathered headdresses, and run out to meet de Vargas and his men as the Spaniards' horses prance down Palace Street.

One of the Indian vendors who sit determinedly under the portal at the Palace as if today were just any day announces, "Here come those Taiwan Indians."

"¡Viva Carlos Segundo! ¡Viva el Rey, Nuestro Señor!" the returning soldiers call. *Long live Charles the Second. Long live the king, our lord.*

Usually it rains a bit, and sometimes that turns the "Indians" white again before the pageant ends. But for all its farcical qualities, and for all the questions the pageant and Fiesta raise, they do succeed in bringing a

Two Ballet Folklorico dancers wait reflectively between performances at Fiesta. Besides providing entertainment, the dance groups help preserve Mexican traditions. They also give young performers a sense of identity and a focus for spare energy and time. And they foster strong family bonds, as parents help their offspring with costumes, rehearsals, and performances.

On Saturday afternoon of Fiesta, amateur performers reenact don Diego de Vargas's peaceful first entrada *to New Mexico in 1692. This preliminary return of the Spanish to New Mexico after the Pueblo Revolt led to today's myth of the peaceful reconquest of New Mexico.*

During Fiesta weekend Ballet Folklorico groups entertain on the plaza. Dressed in traditional folk costumes from Mexico, dancers whirl their skirts and stomp around the dance platform.

fragment of the past into the present. For the children in Fiesta dress who wiggle on their parents' shoulders, for the old women in black shawls who fade back into the crowd, don Diego de Vargas breathes and speaks again.

The two-hundred-acre Rancho de las Golondrinas museum in the Santa Fe suburb of La Cienega also makes history come alive. There, at a Spanish colonial hacienda dating to the early 1700s, volunteers recreate eighteenth- and nineteenth-century daily life during the annual Spring Festival and Harvest Festival, the first weekends in June and October.

A round adobe watchtower, the *torreón,* guards the windowless outer walls of the hacienda. In the sunshine of the inner courtyard, a young woman sits weaving chiles into *ristras,* and an old woman bakes bread in the adobe *horno.* Sometimes musicians play the violin and sing old favorites like "Allá en el rancho grande, allá donde vivía. . . ." *(Over at the big ranch, over where I used to live. . . .)* Out back, an old woman stirs the rendered fat and lye in a big black soap vat over a fire, and an old man in a *tilma* (poncho) leads a burro loaded with wood. Farther on, a woman uses yucca root to wash the oil from freshly shorn wool.

Early Sunday morning during the spring festival, processioners carry a statue of San Isidro, patron saint of agriculture, to a small chapel overlooking the fields. Nearby, hand-carved wooden markers commemorate the dead in a traditional, unkempt village cemetery, the *camposanto.* Inside the *morada* (the Penitente meeting house), a Penitente musician sings wailing, ancient hymns that sound like the Moorish-influenced *saetas* of Andalucía, Spain.

After passing several hours surrounded by the sights, sounds, smells, and tastes of yesterday, it seems almost possible to feel and taste the past. Listening to that mournful singing or the rhythmic dripping of the water off the mill wheel close by, visitors may find themselves aching for the past, or grieving for the present as it fades away.

In mid-afternoon the Matachines dance begins. Bystanders pull back to form an elliptical circle as men in ribboned headdresses step into the dusty dance plaza. The violinist positions his bow, and the Matachines wheel, circle, stamp, and bow to the repetitive music. La Malinche, a girl of about eight dressed in bridal white, weaves among them.

Meanwhile, one of the *abuelos,* two seedy looking characters who wear partial masks and face paint, drags a woman from the crowd to dance a few steps with him beside the Matachines. The other *abuelo* pulls off a little boy's shoe and uses it for a football. Then the first snatches a purse, pulls out the contents, one by one, and displays them to the tittering crowd.

After that, both *abuelos* dive at a young dancer, the *torito.* Dressed as a small bull, the *torito* screams as the *abuelos* pantomime in vivid detail his transformation from bull to steer.

Through all this, the oblivious Matachines wave their three-pronged wooden *palmas* (scepters) as they wind in and out in steps reminiscent of a ribbon dance.

Friday evening of Fiesta a defiant effigy known variously as Zozobra or Old Man Gloom points his finger at the crowd, shakes his enormous head, and moans. When flames run up and down his paper, muslin, and wooden frame, the accumulated sorrows and misfortunes of Santa Feans are said to burn away, too.

At Christmastime debates about the virtues of old Santa Fe versus new fade from roars to whispers as people of all faiths and ethnic backgrounds celebrate together—and borrow cultural themes from each other. These Christmas ornaments in a Santa Fe Christmas shop owe their appeal to their Pueblo Indian motifs.

What exactly is this surrealistic combination of the earnest and the bizarre? On one level, the dance recounts Montezuma's conversion to Christianity almost five centuries ago. On another, it ritualizes the ancient conflict between good and evil. On another, it suggests that nothing is so serious that it can't be made fun of, and nothing is so distracting that it can't be ignored.

The rite also represents the durability of tradition: The Matachines dance is said to have begun in Moorish North Africa two thousand or more years ago, and to have traveled with the Moors to Spain. There it became so much a part of Spanish culture that even after Queen Isabel and King Ferdinand drove out the last Moors in 1492, the dance survived.

Early colonists brought it to the New World, where it merged with native traditions. Meanwhile, Jesuits and other missionaries gave it a Christian overlay. From Mexico the dance traveled north to New Mexico, where the Pueblo Indians adopted it. Today, it survives in the Santa Fe area in both Pueblo and Spanish versions. The *abuelos* in the Spanish version show the influence of Pueblo tradition: One is the Summer *abuelo;* the other is the Winter *abuelo.*

One October afternoon at Rancho de las Golondrinas, after the last violin note had faded, I talked to the Winter *abuelo,* Rudy Herrera. The descendant of early Spanish colonists, he lives north of Santa Fe in the village of Nambé. When Rudy was a child, a Spanish group at El Rancho and an Indian group at "San I'fonso" (San Ildefonso) traded dancers back and forth. Rudy's uncle danced with them. The little boy looked at the men and thought, "If only I could be a Matachines dancer when I grow up. Just a plain dancer. Nothing special." It was too much to hope that he might become an *abuelo.*

Then during the 1950s and 1960s, the men of El Rancho stopped dancing, and it looked as if neither Rudy nor any other young men would grow up to be Matachines. But in the mid-1970s, they decided to revive the dance. They found an old man who had danced with both the El Rancho group and the San Ildefonsos. They located old tape recordings of the music and musicians to play it. Soon the Matachines de El Rancho were reborn. Rudy was chosen to play the *abuelo.*

Although he has a reputation as a gentle, kind man, Rudy also has a look so ferocious it could turn back a posse. When he finished telling me his story, he raised a hairy hand to his long black hair and grinned. "I don't know why they chose me to be the *abuelo.* Maybe it's just my personality."

His wife made a face and dragged him away.

As the crowd wandered out to the dusty parking lot, the late afternoon sunlight glinted on the straw in the mud plaster of the restored hacienda's walls and turned it to gold. If I didn't leave right that moment, I knew, I'd succumb to that malaria-like malady, Santa Fe Mystique-itis.

Still, even Las Golondrinas, even Fiesta, can't compare to Christmas in that respect. During Christmastime, ancient pageants, exotic rituals, holiday foods, and music can most easily seduce onlookers away from objectivity and make them babble mawkishly.

For many Santa Feans, Christmas begins and ends with pageants that date back to the plays of medieval Spain. The first is *Las Posadas,* a folk version of the Biblical tale of Mary and Joseph's search for an inn the night of Christ's birth.

One icy December Sunday evening before Christmas, the plaza fills with spectators waiting for parishioners from Santa Cruz, a village north of Santa Fe, to enact *Las Posadas.* Meanwhile, inside the History Library at the Palace of the Governors, the villagers prepare for the pageant. The young man who plays José (Joseph) adjusts his brown head covering, and the young woman who plays María (Mary) fusses with her long blue wrap. Their companions practice their songs one last time and nibble on a tray of *bizcochitos,* traditional holiday cookies.

Then all the players step out into the night and sing the ritual words, in Spanish, "Who will give these pilgrims lodging?" As spectators press close, the processioners stop at nine points around the plaza, singing their pleas. Again and again, the door slams.

"No."

"Go away."

"It must be robbers."

"If this is the Queen of Heaven, why is she wandering around all alone in the night?"

Meanwhile, on rooftops, two devil figures in red costumes taunt the pilgrims in Gringoish Spanish.

At last, at the ninth stop, María and José hear the welcome words, "Oh is that you, María? Is that you, José? Enter, Holy Pilgrims, enter."

With that, *Las Posadas* ends, and the crowd flows like a tidal wave into the courtyard of the Palace of the Governors. There they warm themselves at bonfires called *luminarias.* They drink hot apple cider and sing traditional Christmas carols in English and Spanish. José and María and the other Santa Cruz parishioners disappear into the old Palace and prepare for the ride back to Santa Cruz. But the two devil figures, who both live in Santa Fe, linger around the fire.

One Christmas Dr. Darrell Dawson, who has played the devil for about fifteen years, addressed the audience gathered at the *luminarias:* "I don't think we should split good and evil like we do." Then he pointed to the white paint he had daubed on his face and twisted his lips in a devilish smile. "Of course, it's probably significant that the devil is often depicted in white face in New Mexico."

Other Christmas-season pageants include *Los Tres Reyes Magos,* the story of the Three Wise Men, and *Los Pastores.* This folk rendition of the

Above: A dance group known as Los Matachines de El Rancho perform the millennia-old Matachines dance at El Rancho de las Golondrinas. The only female dancer, a young girl in white, plays La Malinche. A complex figure from Mexican history who betrayed her people to the Spanish conquistadors, La Malinche has emerged in the folk history of northern New Mexico as a symbol of purity and innocence. During pauses between dance sets, relatives and onlookers pin money to her veil and dress.

Right: On Christmas Eve, homeowners line their rooftops, driveways, and walls with sand-weighted paper bags, each of which holds a candle. Elsewhere these Christmas lights are often called luminarias; *here they are known as* farolitos. *In the Canyon Road–Acequia Madra area, streets close for three hours while an estimated 30,000 strollers enjoy the* farolito *displays.*

Overleaf: Glowing farolitos *transform an ordinary adobe wall into a visual poem on Christmas Eve. According to northern New Mexico folk traditions, the* farolitos *light the way for the* Santo Niño, *the Baby Jesus. With or without religious overtones, their wavering lights rouse the holiday spirit in even the most jaded.*

Above: September's Fiesta ends Sunday night with a candlelight procession from St. Francis Cathedral to Fort Marcy Hill. The hill, at the northeast edge of downtown, represents at least a thousand years of Santa Fe living. In the city's pre-Spanish days, Indians built adobe homes here. After the U.S. took New Mexico from Mexico in 1846, American soldiers built an adobe fortress on the hill. Today you'll find no obvious remains of either that fort or those long-ago Indian homes. Instead, the hilltop Cross of the Martyrs commemorates Franciscans who died during the Pueblo Revolt of 1680.

Left: During the Spanish and Mexican eras and as late as the 1940s vendors traveled with loaded burros and mules from village to village. Here, a wood vendor pauses outside the adobe walls of the old hacienda at El Rancho de las Golondrinas.

Above: In many cases electric farolitos have replaced the old-fashioned candles, sand, and paper bags. Here, electric farolitos light businesses around the plaza.

Right: For logistical reasons, two men alternate playing the devil from one rooftop to the next during the pre-Christmas performance of Las Posadas *on the plaza. After José and María finally find a place to stay, spectators warm themselves in front of bonfires called* luminarias *in the courtyard of the Palace of the Governors. Here, the two devils clown together in front of a* luminaria.

Biblical tale of the shepherds watching their flocks the night of Christ's birth stars a sleepy shepherd, Bartolo. His favorite drink is old-time Wild West firewater—*aguardiente*.

When it's time to go to Belén (Bethlehem) to greet the newborn Christ, Bartolo refuses to budge. Finally the other shepherds sing, "En Belén hay aguardiente, Bartolo." *In Bethlehem there's firewater, Bartolo.* And off they go.

But the real highlight of Christmas, for many Santa Feans, comes on Christmas Eve. Adults and children around town fill plain brown paper lunch bags with enough sand to anchor them in the wind, and place a votive candle in each one. By late afternoon, householders kneel on the edges of their flat-topped roofs and position these homemade Christmas lights at intervals all around. As the light fades and the temperature falls below freezing, and the air fills with the smell of piñon burning in fireplaces, the *farolitos,* as Santa Feans call them, begin glowing all over town.

Nowhere is the show more spectacular than in the Canyon Road and Acequia Madre areas, where a thousand *farolitos* and more may line the roof, walls, and driveway of each business or home. Sometimes it snows, or an icy wind blows. But still, thousands of Christmas Eve strollers turn out. They gaze dreamily at the *farolitos.* They warm feet, hands, and faces around juniper *luminarias.* They make friendly jokes explaining why, in other Southwest cities, *farolitos* are called *luminarias* and *luminarias* are just called bonfires. Some ponder the old northern New Mexico legend that the true purpose of the *farolitos* and *luminarias* is to light the path for the Santo Niño, the Christ Child. Others remember a different folk tale of the *farolitos'* origin: that they began as paper lanterns in China and arrived in the New World on the Manila galleons of the 1600s.

As people wander through the narrow streets, they form spontaneous groups and sing Christmas carols, from "Silent Night" to "Vamos Todos a Belén." They accept cups of hot cider from homeowners who ladle it from large black cauldrons. They breathe in the aromas of the Christmas *posole* simmering on stovetops all over town. And the more they walk, the more they sing, the more they watch, and the more they listen, the more Christmas seems like Christmas.

Even Scrooge would soften if he could visit Santa Fe on Christmas Eve.

In the Santa Fe suburb of La Cienega, the two-century-old Rancho de las Golondrinas has become a living museum. During weekend festivals each spring and fall, volunteers reenact customs from Spanish colonial, Mexican, and territorial times. On a hillside beyond the hacienda compound, the Sierra Village replicates a traditional New Mexico mountain village. Here, flowers bloom in front of the casa de la abuelita, the grandmother's house. After the grandfather died, families would commonly choose one child to go live with the widowed grandmother and keep her company.

Wild Rivers and
Wild Flowers:
Outdoors

In the January 1, 1910, issue of the Santa Fe *New Mexican,* the Santa Fe Board of Trade tried to attract newcomers by playing up the city's outdoor splendors.

"Why locate in Santa Fe County?" one advertisement asked. "Because it has nature's blessing." Santa Fe was "the healthiest health resort in the United States" and "the city of a thousand wonders," with "unrivaled scenery and places for ideal outings." It was "cool in summer, sunny in winter, bracing the year around."

Not everyone agreed. Two decades earlier, on July 1, 1889, Swiss-born scholar Adolph Bandelier spoke for Santa Fe's detractors when he wrote in his journal, "Let anybody speak to me of the 'Climate of Santa Fe.' It is the meanest, the most abject, the dryest, the most abjectly windy spot upon earth. Not fit for people to honor it with their presence. Not a single man or woman can live here unless he is in a dying condition, when it may occur that the hellish, fiendish winds blowing here, give him some strength through the gymnastics they force upon his lungs."

Maybe it was an especially windy year, or maybe Bandelier was just having a bad day. Then again, maybe he was right.

In a one-hundred-mile radius around Santa Fe, the countryside ranges from treeless flatlands to mountain meadows and includes over two million acres of public land. Outdoor activities are nearly endless. You can fish for trout in the Pecos River or pull catfish out of Cochiti Lake. You can hunt deer in the pine woods of Santa Fe National Forest, ski down snowy mountaintops twelve thousand feet high, or hike among canyons, mesas, and federal wildernesses.

You can kayak through rapids on the Río Grande or bet on horses at the Santa Fe Downs. You can study birds or photograph wildflowers. You can watch golden aspen leaves quiver against the blue September sky. You can pick through the gravel near Mount Chalchihuitl for bits of native turquoise, or swirl the sand in a water-filled pan and watch for the gleam of gold. If you had happened to be at the right place in the 1980s, you could even have witnessed masked bandidos robbing a gold mine south of town or have watched a mounted posse track down a desperado.

But there's one thing you can't do, and that is to predict accurately

The moon rises over an abandoned house near the old mining village of Cerrillos, south of Santa Fe. For centuries before Europeans arrived, Indians mined turquoise near here. Through an elaborate network of trails, the turquoise passed from trader to trader and tribe to tribe, all the way to Central America and beyond. Today the Cerrillos turquoise mines are closed to visitors, but pebbles of the greenish blue mineral sometimes lie among the gravel on nearby roads.

how a stranger, or a group of strangers, will react to the land around Santa Fe, or how their reactions will change as the countryside pulses around them. Like so much else about Santa Fe, the outdoors elicits the widest possible range of responses.

Take my friend Angela, an artist and television producer. When she moved to New Mexico from Germany six years ago, the mesas and sparsely covered hills intimidated her. Where others saw poetry in the red rocks, sloping plains, and granite mountainsides, she saw only bare, open, naked spaces. They made her feel lonely, even desolate.

"There's no oasis for my eyes," she complained, "and no oasis for my feelings."

One day, I made things worse when I reminded her to watch out for rattlesnakes as we tromped across the countryside. Then she read in a newspaper about a Santa Fe man who nearly died of bubonic plague, a disease still endemic throughout the desert Southwest.

Angela longed for the safety of city streets and the security of crowds. Gradually, though, she became acquainted with her enemy.

She traveled the back road between Santa Fe and Albuquerque, known as the Turquoise Trail, and listened to a silence she had never heard before: no cars, no people, no airplanes, no trucks. Just the sound of a raven flapping its wings, and the movement of the breeze among the globemallows and asters.

She drove northwest of Santa Fe to Bandelier National Monument, named for Adolph Bandelier. There she sat in a prehistoric cave and imagined the people who lived in Frijoles Canyon hundreds of years ago, men and women who sat where she now sat, studying the shadows and the seasons as they changed.

She watched summer rainstorms and winter snowstorms and saw double and triple rainbows arch across the sky.

Bit by bit, her perceptions of the outdoors changed. "Now I love it all, especially the sky," she says. "It's the most beautiful sky in the world. It makes you dream. It's like a movie, always changing. It has wonderful colors, and you can lose yourself in the openness of the sky."

Of course, Angela still doesn't like the thought of stepping on a rattlesnake. And she hopes never to have to tell her mother, back in Cologne, that she has caught the plague. But she understands now that rattlesnakes don't sit around waiting for someone to sharpen their fangs on. And she knows that as long as she stays away from dead animals and keeps a flea collar on her cat, she's more likely to be smashed by a plummeting hot-air balloon than to be bit by a plague-carrying flea.

Myself, I like to hike among the conical Tent Rocks at Cochiti Pueblo down by the Río Grande. Or pick wild raspberries along Big Tesuque Trail in the mountains above Santa Fe. Or try to decipher petroglyphs. Or wander through back-road cemeteries filled with weeds and homemade crosses.

If one flower symbolizes old Santa Fe, it's the hollyhock, which blooms all summer long. According to Spanish colonial tradition, Joseph's staff sprouted hollyhock blossoms when he was chosen as Mary's spouse. In the Spanish villages of northern New Mexico, hollyhocks retain the name varas de San José: St. Joseph's staffs.

Often in these hidden burial grounds no marker bears a name, yet none of the dead are forgotten.

But there's no weekend retreat more soothing than an escape to the Bisti Badlands, about a three-hour drive northwest of Santa Fe. There, in a four-thousand-acre federal wilderness area, dinosaur bones and petrified wood emerge from the hard-packed sand. Twisting mudstone and sandstone formations rise like Martian landscapes into the empty sky. You can walk all day without seeing another person. But golden eagles fly, mourning doves sing, and lizards rush across the hot desert floor, leaving tiny footprints in the sand.

One night after staying to watch the late afternoon sun turn the badlands into a study in light and shadow, my partner and I waited until dark to walk the two miles back to the car. No moon shone, but the Milky Way spread out above us like a fishnet full of lights pinned to the sky. They glowed so brightly that we could find our way without a flashlight.

Slowly we returned past dark pillars and columns, and it seemed as if we had stepped into a poetic tale of adventure travel from some bygone day, perhaps an account by French writer Antoine de Saint-Exupéry or a travel story by one of the German romantic poets of the last century. Or maybe even a recent tale of desert mysticism by Carlos Castaneda.

As we moved silently through the darkness, owls hooted off to our right and left. Then, as if on signal, coyotes on a nearby mesatop began their nocturnal concert. First a lone voice warbled a protracted howl. Then coyote after coyote added a plaintive song, until the desert echoed. But this crescendo signaled the end. One by one, the singers dropped out, until finally only the voice of the lone coyote chorus-master remained. Then he, too, stopped, and the night was silent.

In the city of Santa Fe you can also see, hear, and study the rhythms of the high desert, or, more accurately, the edge of the high desert. Santa Fe is generally considered to be near, but not really part of, the state's two deserts, the Chihuahuan Desert and the Great Basin Desert.

During its long winters, which often last a full half year, Santa Fe more closely resembles the cold-wintered Great Basin. The first snow falls in the city in October, and old-timers like to scare newcomers with the saying, "It always snows in April, and it may snow in May." Then they talk about the time, years ago, when two feet of snow fell in June. But for every winter with a total snowfall in the city of four feet, there's another winter with a total snowfall of less than a foot. All winter long, the sun usually evaporates snow within a few days, and before and after storms the sky stays so blue that there's no such thing as winter gloom. Observes part-time Santa Fe resident Bill Ashbey, who moved here from New Jersey and recently spent his first winter here, "This is the only winter I ever remember when I wasn't longing for spring."

After scarcely a week of spring, winter becomes summer. Lilacs bloom

Six centuries ago, the ancestors of today's Pueblo Indians planted corn, beans, and squash near their mud homes at Bandelier National Monument in Frijoles Canyon west of Santa Fe. Then as now, caves pocked the hillsides. Nineteenth-century scholar Adolph Bandelier set his classic novel of pre-historic Indian life, The Delight Makers, *here. Today seventy miles of hiking trails cross the 37,000-acre national monument named in his honor. Pueblo Indians still make pilgrimages to shrines in these mountains, and ninety percent of the park remains undisturbed wilderness.*

Above: After the U.S. took over New Mexico in 1846, Santa Fe served as the military headquarters of New Mexico. But because the capital was considered a "sink of vice and extravagance," Fort Union was built to replace it in 1851. Today Santa Fe endures, along with its vices and extravagances, and Fort Union has become a national monument, filled with adobe ruins and ghosts.

Left: Federal, state, and Indian lands surround Santa Fe like a cushion and protect the city from excessive growth. Here, snakeweed glows in the late afternoon light along a back road on Santo Domingo Pueblo land south of Santa Fe. The Ortiz Mountains rise in the background. Common throughout the Southwest, snakeweed grows on over-grazed rangelands.

Overleaf: Throughout northern New Mexico, backroad travelers encounter rustic village cemeteries known as camposantos. *Here, the slanting light of a winter afternoon shines on simple homemade crosses and a wooden grave enclosure in the Spanish village of Vadito along the High Road to Taos. In the background, snow highlights Truchas Peaks in the Sangre de Cristo Mountains.*

Above: For centuries the Indians of New Mexico pecked petroglyphs into the rocks around Santa Fe. Today scholars debate their meanings, and each tribe interprets the rock art according to its own traditions. Most agree, though, that the musician playing what looks like a trumpet represents Kokopelli, the hunchbacked flute player of Pueblo Indian legends.

Below: Near the village of Cochiti Pueblo, west of Santa Fe, wind and water have carved the hills into pinnacles called Tent Rocks. Even seasoned hikers sometimes get lost. Author Susan Hazen-Hammond and her photographer partner Eduardo Fuss like to tell the story about the time, one dry summer day, when they hiked in a narrow, winding canyon. He went ahead to take pictures; she followed with the water. Then he climbed to the canyon rim, confident he'd see her. But he didn't. She passed him without knowing it, and hiked all the way to the mouth of the canyon before she realized she'd missed him. "I thought I was going to die of thirst before she found me," he says. "That taught me a lesson. I don't care how heavy the camera bag is; I always carry my own water."

Overleaf: All winter long ice in frozen ponds and streams around Santa Fe creates nature's own frozen art gallery. It often surprises newcomers to learn that winter lasts half a year. Winters have been generally mild in this century, but earlier writers talk of the Río Grande freezing so solid that wagons could cross it. One exasperated seventeenth-century observer described the climate in northern New Mexico as "eight months of winter and four months of hell."

and insects buzz. By June, the rainy season begins, with clear mornings, afternoon thunderstorms, and mild nights. Whereas the temperature falls below freezing an average of 150 days each winter, it rises above 90 degrees Fahrenheit only seven days each summer.

Yet in spite of these known weather patterns, the unexpected is almost the norm. And the longer people live in Santa Fe, the more they become aware of the influence the weather has on the creatures that live in their gardens.

One recent springtime, for instance, the weather stayed cold later than usual. But the two pairs of sparrows that nest each year in the rain gutters in our patio flew back and forth with twigs and grasses and wove their nests anyway. One couple built close to the house; the other built way out at the end of the gutter at the far corner of the patio.

One late May evening I stepped outside and heard the faint cheeping of newly hatched chicks in the closer nest. But the eggs in the other nest didn't hatch, even though the mother continued to sit on them day after day. We wondered if the unseasonal cold had killed them one night, and the mother didn't know.

Then, unexpectedly early and unexpectedly hard, it rained. Big, pelting drops the size of marbles splattered on sidewalks and tore at the evening primroses. The streets turned into extemporaneous arroyos, as if nature were reminding us that these lanes, after all, had once been dry streambeds and could be reclaimed as streambeds any time.

As the water filled the rain gutters, the mother of the chicks that had hatched flew in and out, twittering desperately. Her babies were too young to fly and too big for her to carry to safety. She and her mate could save only themselves. She sang to her children, she called to them, but one by one the rain submerged them, and their squeaky voices stopped.

Meanwhile, the other mother, whose eggs had not hatched, stayed determinedly at her post. The water rose, but still she did not leave them, even as she drowned.

When the sun came out the next day, her mate sang heartbrokenly, then flew away.

At first the mother and father of the chicks that had drowned couldn't believe their babies had died. They called, they sang, they looked up and down the gutter. But finally one morning their song changed from puzzlement to grief. They mourned for several days, then flew away.

Even wilderness animals sometimes find their way into the city. One year a young mountain lion scampered into a back yard on the north side of Santa Fe. Recently, a blonde-haired black bear looked through the window of another northside home. Last summer a skunk passed unexpectedly through our own neighborhood. And once about every three years a roadrunner shows up in our back yard. With long tail and spotted crest, he runs from one yard to the next and hops up and down over walls for several days. Then he disappears.

But probably nothing can beat the horny toads—properly called short-horned lizards—in their ability to turn Santa Fe homeowners into amateur naturalists. Each spring these scaly creatures emerge from their winter burrows so skinny and weak that they can hardly stick out their tongues to nab a passing ant. But soon they fatten up, and the females begin swelling.

About the time the first hollyhocks bloom, in late June or early July, the mothers give birth to litters of six or more baby lizards. As her nickel-sized purple newborns tumble around the yard, the mother horned toad finds a place on high ground where she can survey her offspring's antics and guard them against neighborhood cats. By the time the hummingbirds arrive in August, the babies have taken on the coloration of their chosen territories and have eaten many times their weight in ants.

Spring lilacs, summer storms, autumn leaves, winter snows. Life, death, life again. Mountaintops, river valleys, moonscapes, and lizards. They all roll together until after a while, it sometimes gets to seeming as if this were the only place on earth worth passing one's days.

Most Santa Feans I know would sympathize with a young man named David whose parents decided to leave Santa Fe and move to Indiana a few years ago.

David didn't want to go, so his father tried to lure him away with accounts of the wonders of Indiana. "But there's grass there everywhere, David. And everything's wet and green."

"But, Dad," wailed the boy. "I like it brown and dry."

Only in Santa Fe.

Short-horned lizards, commonly called horny toads, live in desert-landscaped yards throughout Santa Fe. They've also become part of Santa Fe kitsch: Gold- and silver-plated metal horny toads sometimes decorate car hoods. The perfect non-pet pet, horned lizards need no care or attention and grow fat and friendly eating ants. Here, a horned lizard rests on a weathered log in the author's back yard.

Above: In Santa Fe National Forest high in the Sangre de Cristo Mountains above Santa Fe, Big Tesuque Creek rushes over downed logs, tempting passing artists to pick up camera or sketchpad. Throughout the summer, hikers wander along trails in the mountainous forest. In the autumn, sightseers by the hundreds drive up Hyde Park Road to view the golden aspen leaves. During the winter, sunshine warms the snow-chilled mountain air, even at elevations of ten thousand and twelve thousand feet. Between Thanksgiving Day and mid-April, 200,000 skiers swoosh down the thirty-eight ski trails at the Santa Fe Ski Area.

Above left: Once each year, during the Balloon Fiesta in October, Albuquerque outshines Santa Fe as a tourist attraction. More than 750,000 spectators come to watch hot air balloons billow up and rise into the sky during the nine-day event.

Below left: The Albuquerque Balloon Fiesta attracts an estimated one thousand amateur and professional photographers for each of the more than five hundred hot air balloons, earning it a reputation as the most heavily photographed event on earth. Here, a few of the hardiest camera carriers line up against the morning sky.

For Further Reading

▼▼▼▼▼▼▼▼▼▼▼▼▼▼▼▼▼▼▼▼▼▼▼▼

Arnold, Sam'l P. *Eating Up the Santa Fe Trail*. Niwot, Colorado: University Press of Colorado, 1990.

Bandelier, Adolf. *The Delight Makers*. New York: Harcourt Brace Jovanovich, 1971.

Bloom, Lansing B., ed., "A Trade-Invoice of 1638," *New Mexico Historical Review,* July 1935, pp. 242–48.

Boyd, E. *Popular Arts of Spanish New Mexico*. Santa Fe: Museum of New Mexico Press, 1974.

Brody, J. J. *Anasazi and Pueblo Painting*. Albuquerque: University of New Mexico Press, 1991.

Bunting, Bainbridge. *John Gaw Meem: Southwestern Architect*. Albuquerque: University of New Mexico Press for the School of American Research, 1983.

Bunting, Bainbridge. *Of Earth and Timbers Made: New Mexico Architecture*. Albuquerque: University of New Mexico Press, 1974.

Campa, Arthur L. *Hispanic Culture in the Southwest*. Norman, Oklahoma: University of Oklahoma Press, 1979.

Carroll, H. Bailey, and J. Villasana Haggard, trans. *Three New Mexico Chronicles: The Exposición of Don Pedro Bautista Pino 1812; the Ojeada of Lic. Antonio Barreiro 1832; and the Additions by Don José Agustín de Escudero, 1849*. New York: Arno Press, 1967.

Champe, Flavia. *The Matachines Dance of the Upper Rio Grande: History, Music, and Choreography*. Lincoln, Nebraska: The University of Nebraska Press, 1983.

Chávez, Fray Angélico. *My Penitente Land: Reflections on Spanish New Mexico*. Albuquerque: University of New Mexico Press, 1974.

Coke, Van Deren. *Taos and Santa Fe: The Artist's Environment, 1882–1942*. Albuquerque: University of New Mexico Press, et al., 1963.

Day Hikes in the Santa Fe Area, Third Edition. Santa Fe Group of the Sierra Club, 1990.

Dent, Huntley. *The Feast of Santa Fe*. New York: Simon and Schuster, 1985.

Elliott, Michael L. *The Archeology of Santa Fe: A Background Report*. City of Santa Fe, 1988.

Ellis, Bruce. *Bishop Lamy's Santa Fe Cathedral*. Albuquerque: University of New Mexico Press, 1985.

Espinosa, José E. *Saints in the Valleys: Christian Sacred Images in the History, Life and Folk Art of Spanish New Mexico,* Revised Edition. Albuquerque: University of New Mexico Press, 1967.

Fergusson, Erna. *New Mexico: A Pageant of Three Peoples*. Albuquerque: University of New Mexico Press, 1985.

Fink, Augusta. *I–Mary: A Biography of Mary Austin*. Tucson: University of Arizona Press, 1983.

Freeman, Martha Doty, "New Mexico in the Nineteenth Century: The Creation of an Artistic Tradition," *New Mexico Historical Review,* January 1974, pp. 5–26.

Gish, Robert. "'Pretty, But Is It History?' The Legacy of Harvey Fergusson's Rio Grande," *New Mexico Historical Review,* April 1985, pp. 173–92.

Gregg, Josiah. *Commerce of the Prairies,* ed. by Max Moorhead. Norman: University of Oklahoma Press, 1954.

Hammond, George P., "The Zuñiga Journal, Tucson to Santa Fé: The Opening of a Spanish Trade Route, 1788–1795," *New Mexico Historical Review,* January 1931, pp. 40–65.

Hazen-Hammond, Susan. *A Short History of Santa Fe*. San Francisco: Lexikos Press, 1988.

Hillerman, Tony, ed. *The Spell of New Mexico*. Albuquerque: University of New Mexico Press, 1984.

Historical District Handbook: A Guide to Architectural Preservation and Design Regulations in Santa Fe's Five Historic Districts. City of Santa Fe, 1986.

[Holmes, Ruth, ed.] *Old Santa Fe Today*. Albuquerque: University of New Mexico Press for the Historic Santa Fe Foundation, Fourth Edition, 1991.

Horgan, Paul. *The Centuries of Santa Fe*. Santa Fe: Gannon, 1976.

Horgan, Paul. *Lamy of Santa Fe: His Life and Times*. New York: Farrar, Straus & Giroux, 1975.

Hughes, Phyllis, ed. *Pueblo Indian Cookbook*. Santa Fe: Museum of New Mexico Press, 1977.

Ingersoll, Raymond V., ed. *Archaeology*

Beadwork on this Plains headdress displayed at Indian Market reflects the many hours of labor that go into making a traditional costume.

and History of Santa Fe Country. New Mexico Geological Society, Special Publication No. 8, 1979.

Jones, Oakah L., "Lew Wallace: Hoosier Governor of Territorial New Mexico, 1878–81," New Mexico Historical Review, April 1985, pp. 145–58.

Keleher, William A. Turmoil in New Mexico 1846–1868. Albuquerque: University of New Mexico Press, 1982.

Kessell, John L. Kiva, Cross, and Crown: The Pecos Indians and New Mexico 1540–1840. Washington, DC: U.S. Department of the Interior, 1987.

Kessell, John L., ed. Remote Beyond Compare: Letters of don Diego de Vargas to His Family from New Spain and New Mexico 1675–1706. Albuquerque: University of New Mexico Press, 1989.

La Farge, Oliver, and Arthur N. Morgan. Santa Fe: Autobiography of a Southwestern Town. Norman: University of Oklahoma Press, 1985.

Macrae, Laurie. Santa Fe Public Library Select Southwest Bibliography. Santa Fe: Sunstone, 1989.

Mather, Christine, and Sharon Woods. Santa Fe Style. New York: Rizzoli, 1986.

Miller, Mark Charles. Coyote Café: Foods from the Great Southwest. Berkeley: Ten Speed Press, 1989.

Moorhead, Max L. New Mexico's Royal Road: Trade and Travel on the Chihuahua Trail. Norman, Oklahoma: University of Oklahoma Press, 1958.

Nestor, Sarah. The Native Market of the Spanish New Mexican Craftsmen: Santa Fe, 1933–1940. Santa Fe: Colonial New Mexico Historical Foundation, 1978.

Niethammer, Carolyn J. The Tumbleweed Gourmet: Cooking with Wild Southwestern Plants. Tucson: University of Arizona Press, 1987.

Noble, David Grant, ed. Santa Fe: History of an Ancient City. Santa Fe: School of American Research Press, 1989.

Ortiz, Alfonso. The Tewa World: Space, Time, Being, and Becoming in a Pueblo Society. Chicago: University of Chicago Press, 1969.

Patterson-Rudolph, Carol. Petroglyphs and Pueblo Myths of the Rio Grande. Albuquerque: Avanyu Publishing, 1990.

Reeve, Agnesa Lufkin. From Hacienda to Bungalow: Northern New Mexico Houses, 1850–1912. Albuquerque: University of New Mexico Press, 1988.

Robertson, Edna C. Los Cinco Pintores. Santa Fe: Museum of New Mexico, 1975.

Robertson, Edna C., and Sarah Nestor. Artists of the Canyons and Caminos: Santa Fe, the Early Years. Peregrine Smith, 1976.

Santa Fe Historic Neighborhood Study. City of Santa Fe: 1988.

Scheinbaum, David. Bisti. Albuquerque: University of New Mexico Press, 1987.

Scott, Eleanor. The First Twenty Years of the Santa Fe Opera. Santa Fe: Sunstone Press, 1976.

Sheppard, Carl D. Creator of the Santa Fe Style: Isaac Hamilton Rapp, Architect. Albuquerque: University of New Mexico Press, 1988.

Sherman, John. Santa Fe: A Pictorial History. Norfolk, Virginia: Donning Company, 1983.

Shishkin, J. K. The Palace of the Governors. Santa Fe: Museum of New Mexico Press, 1972.

Simmons, Marc, ed. On the Santa Fe Trail. Lawrence, Kansas: University Press of Kansas, 1986.

Simmons, Marc. Yesterday in Santa Fe. Santa Fe: Sunstone, 1989.

Snow, Cordelia Thomas, "A Brief History of the Palace of the Governors and a Preliminary Report on the 1974 Excavation," El Palacio, Fall 1974, pp. 1–22.

Tigges, Linda, ed. Santa Fe Historic Plaza Study I with Translations from Spanish Colonial Documents. Santa Fe: City Planning Department, 1990.

Vigil, Ralph H., "Willa Cather and Historical Reality," New Mexico Historical Review, April 1975, pp. 123–38.

Weigle, Marta. Brothers of Light, Brothers of Blood: The Penitentes of the Southwest. Albuquerque: University of New Mexico Press, 1976.

For Further Information

New Mexico
Department of Tourism
491 Old Santa Fe Trail
Santa Fe, NM 87503
800-545-2040 or 505-827-7400

Santa Fe
Convention and Visitors Bureau
P.O. Box 909
Santa Fe, NM 87504
800-777-2489 or 505-984-6760

About the Author

Former National Merit Scholar Susan Hazen-Hammond writes nonfiction, poetry, and fiction from her home in Santa Fe. Some of her more than three hundred published articles, reviews, short stories, and poems have been translated into as many as fifteen languages.

A member of Western Writers of America and PEN Center USA West, she has been writing about the Southwest and the Spanish-speaking world for the past dozen years for such publications as *Discovery, Arizona Highways,* and *Reader's Digest*. Her other nonfiction books set in New Mexico are *Enchanting New Mexico* and *A Short History of Santa Fe*. She and photographer Eduardo Fuss work as a team and have traveled together on assignments in Europe, South America, Mexico, and across the U.S.

About the Photographer

Photo by Susan Hazen-Hammond.

Argentine-born photographer Eduardo Fuss fell in love with Santa Fe while passing through in 1978 and moved to the city from Westchester County, New York, in 1980. The former curator of the Joseph Hirshhorn private art collection, he has exhibited his own art and photography in museums and galleries in New York, Connecticut, Maryland, and Maine. His travel and nature photography has appeared in more than a dozen books, and his photographs are published regularly in such magazines as *Smithsonian, Modern Maturity,* and *Arizona Highways*. A major Italian publication, *Airone,* has called him a "Poet of the Visual Image." A member of the American Society of Magazine Photographers (ASMP), he is known world-wide as "The Iceman" for his art photography of the patterns and natural compositions found in lake and pond ice.

Overleaf: Navajo rugs and rug designs have become an essential part of Santa Fe Style.